NEW EUROPEAN IDENTITY AND CITIZENSHIP

This book is part of a research program financed by a grant from the Ford Foundation

New European Identity and Citizenship

Edited by

RÉMY LEVEAU
KHADIJA MOHSEN-FINAN
and
CATHERINE WIHTOL DE WENDEN

LONDON AND NEW YORK

First published 2002 by Ashgate Publishing

Reissued 2018 by Routledge
2 Park Square, Milton Park, Abingdon, Oxon OX14 4RN
711 Third Avenue, New York, NY 10017, USA

Routledge is an imprint of the Taylor & Francis Group, an informa business

Copyright © Rémy Leveau, Khadija Mohsen-Finan, Catherine Wihtol de Wenden 2002

The editors have asserted their moral right under the Copyright, Designs and Patents Act, 1988, to be identified as the editors of this work.

All rights reserved. No part of this book may be reprinted or reproduced or utilised in any form or by any electronic, mechanical, or other means, now known or hereafter invented, including photocopying and recording, or in any information storage or retrieval system, without permission in writing from the publishers.

Notice:
Product or corporate names may be trademarks or registered trademarks, and are used only for identification and explanation without intent to infringe.

Publisher's Note
The publisher has gone to great lengths to ensure the quality of this reprint but points out that some imperfections in the original copies may be apparent.

Disclaimer
The publisher has made every effort to trace copyright holders and welcomes correspondence from those they have been unable to contact.

Ifri (Institut français des relatios internationales) is a research centre and a forum for debate on major international political and economic issues. Headed by Thierry de Montbrial since its founding in 1979, Ifri is a non-profit organization. Its office is in Paris.

The opinions expressed in this book are the responsibility of the authors alone.

A Library of Congress record exists under LC control number: 2002074459

ISBN 13: 978-1-138-71786-2 (hbk)
ISBN 13: 978-1-138-71784-8 (pbk)
ISBN 13: 978-1-315-19617-6 (ebk)

Contents

List of Contributors

Stefano ALLIEVI
Research Fellow, Universita degli studi di Padova,
Italy

Karima IMTIAZ
Senior Lecturer, Centre for the Study of Islam and Christian-Muslims Relations,
Great Britain

Danièle JOLY
Director, Centre for Research on Ethnic Relations, University of Warwick,
Great Britain

Riva KASTORYANO
Research Fellow, Centre national de la recherche scientifique (CNRS)/Centre d'études et de recherches internationales (CERI),
France

Rémy LEVEAU
Professor, Institut d'études politiques de Paris,
Scientific Advisor, Insitut français des relations internationales (Ifri),
France

Bernabé LÓPEZ GARCÍA
Professor, Universidad Autonoma de Madrid,
Spain

Marco MARTINIELLO
Senior Research Fellow and Senior Lecturer,
Centre d'études de l'ethnicité et des migrations (CEDEM),
Belgique

Khadija MOHSEN-FINAN
Research Fellow, Insitut français des relations internationales (Ifri),
France

Vassoodeven VUDDAMALAY
Research Fellow, Université d'Evry,
France

Catherine WIHTOL DE WENDEN
Senior Research Fellow, Centre national de la recherche scientifique (CNRS)/Centre d'études et de recherches internationales (CERI), France

Introduction

Rémy Leveau
Khadija Mohsen-Finan
Catherine Wihtol de Wenden

European countries are handling in different ways the new attitudes towards citizenship and identity that immigrants bring with them.

France continues to absorb immigrants by offering them individual citizenship and refusing to recognise public expression of their collective identity. In the United Kingdom, ethnic community organisations are more politically and socially accepted, even if they do not have full legal status.

But all these paths to integration are now being threatened by strong assertions of identity that are weakening nation-states. In several European Union countries, for example, direct relationships are developing between their regions and the EU. The European Court of Justice has been receiving complaints, especially concerning human rights, from individuals against their own countries. Such developments could undermine national sovereignty in the face of demands for a new, negotiated citizenship.

The policy of assimilation as a way of more effectively absorbing immigrants is now being challenged. By making nationalistic or cultural-religious demands, Corsicans and Muslims are showing that loyalty to an island or religion does not conflict with having French citizenship.

As it seeks to establish itself, European citizenship is acquiring its own internal borders in the shape of the Other – the non-European, the Muslim and people who are marginalized. So a split is growing inside the EU, between Europeans who can move around and live and work where they want and non-Europeans who need entry and residence visas. This is leading to discriminatory treatment of social groups based on their personal situations.

In terms of law and representation, many people from former French and British colonies see the new European political entity as a step backwards from the freedom of movement they inherited from colonial times. A new 'fortress Europe' is being built that excludes less well-off people suspected of having multiple allegiances. To cope with these differences, Europe will have to devise means of regulation that go beyond those of individual states.

While the current immigration to Europe is here to stay, it is also diversifying and breaking free of its colonial past. New host countries that were once simply sources of immigrants – Italy, Spain, Portugal and Greece – are now faced with people they have little or no historic or cultural links with and also new kinds of immigrants, such as women, children who arrive by themselves, unsuccessful asylum-seekers, educated middle-class youngsters, intellectuals and technicians. These newcomers have created immigrant networks that give them a transnational mobility. As the new century begins, a situation of 'migratory flows,'[1] a new universalism involving new political configurations, is developing, despite the routine existence of visas and passports, as well as reaffirmation of the right to emigrate when authoritarian regimes fall or weaken (in southern and eastern Europe, but also in Latin America and Asia) – even if the right of entry is far from guaranteed – based more on the issues of globalisation and human rights than on solidarity between communities.

At the same time, restrictive, dissuasive and sometimes repressive policies by host countries have caused problems, of which undocumented aliens are the most obvious. But the softening European line on the goal of zero immigration (the Tampere summit in October 1999), the realisation that Europe's ageing population will mean a labour shortage by 2020 (reports by the United Nations and the International Labour Organisation in the spring of 2000) and the debates in Spain and Germany about whether to reopen doors to immigration as and when needed have helped immigrants argue against curbs on free movement and access to rights.

The new host countries (Italy, Spain, Portugal and Greece) are the ones that are regularizing immigrants, often urgently, so as to relieve growing pressure of arriving immigrants as the situation demands, including Italy (in 1986, 1990, 1995 and 1998), Spain (1991, 1996 and 2000), Portugal (1993 and 1996) and Greece (1997). But other European countries have done so too – France (1981 and 1997) and Belgium (2000), even if in some countries, such as Germany, illegal immigration is something not discussed.[2] In between times, makeshift situations develop that are handled in various ways, often case by case, through granting temporary status, humanitarian residence permits, temporary asylum, short-term labour contracts or keeping people in limbo, neither able to be regularized or be deported.

In the new countries of origin, such as China, sub-Saharan Africa and Romania, admiration for Europe, which is seen as a land of human rights, the welfare state and source of (illegal) jobs, is the chief spur for emigration. So Romanian peasants are anticipating the enlargement of the European Union by already going back and forth, enthusiastically calling themselves 'Europeans' and trying to keep their names out of the Schengen Information System (SIS) files. The goal is to be 'clean' in the computer, while claiming the right to move around freely.[3]

The kind of citizenship this produces is multiple, but also new in that it enriches standard citizenship with new forms of collective action, new players and

[1] A term used by E. Ma Mung (of Migrinter).

[2] See H. Stobbe, 'Undocumented Migration in the USA and Germany,' *Working Paper*, Center for Comparative Immigration Studies, University of California, San Diego, February 2000.

[3] See R. -M. Lagrave, and D. Diminescu, 'Faire une saison. Pour une anthropologie des migrations roumaines en France; le cas du pays d'Oas,' *Migrations études*, n°91, Nov.-Dec. 1999. See also, for a description of legalised immigrants in France, G. Neyrand, 'Le suivi social des étrangers régularisés en France,' *Migrations études*, n°92, Jan.-Feb. 2000.

new kinds of solidarity that bring autonomy and individual emancipation since, in the final resort, it is a simple matter of having one's papers. Like other disadvantaged people (those without a home or a job), undocumented aliens highlight the no-go areas of civil society. As they emerge from exclusion, more flexible in their activities than more institutionalised groups, their leaders seek links with other excluded groups, working together and throwing off the image of passive social rejects.[4]

The European immigrant scene is steadily growing and changing, sometimes requiring tough measures as well as adjustments and regulation, and going as far as demanding (in Spain, Italy and Germany) the setting up of a federal immigration authority and police to lead the battle against illegal immigrants and clandestine employment rackets, thus further entrenching and legitimising the Schengen system. What are the indirect effects on the internal and external immigrant situation of this shared edifice that is now an established part of a European system that preserves diversity?

The countries of southern Europe – former sources of immigrants and now the new frontiers of the European Union – are having trouble accepting their new role of hosts to immigrants. In northern Europe, debate focuses on models of absorbing immigrants that are shaped by the nature of each country. Since they cannot turn their own models into universal ones, these northern states work out how much they want to preserve and how to do so freely.

France's memory of its colonial past is a key part of its relationship with North African immigrants, especially those from Algeria. Since French nationality is based on both parents being French-born, a person born in France of parents both born in Algeria before independence in 1963 is automatically French at birth.[5] So the relationship of Algerians with French nationality goes back to colonial times, when citizenship was granted under a kind of flexible apartheid regime where one French settler was worth a dozen 'natives' in the electoral system.

This still-fresh memory for both sides silently underpins the relationship between Algerians and French citizenship in an immigrant community that mostly developed after independence. In mainland France, French nationality has become a useful 'vaccination against deportation' for immigrants who settle permanently, bring over their families, have fewer and fewer links with their countries of origin yet still hesitate to seek the nationality of the former colonial power, while passively accepting it when the formalities are made easy. Such changes in behaviour and attitudes lead to a situation of double nationality, especially since Algerian law, as in most Muslim Arab countries, is based on the law of blood and on perpetual allegiance. But since they cannot prevent it, the two countries tolerate

[4] See J. Guilhaumou, 'La citoyenneté à l'épreuve de l'exclusion. Approche historique et comparative,' *Les cahiers de l'Actif*, n°272-273, Jan.-Feb. 1999. See also J. Simeant, *La cause des sans papiers*. Paris, Presses de Sciences Po, 1998, and M. Dridi, 'La lutte des sans papiers et le mouvement associatif 1993,' n°1, May 1997 (*Working Papers*, FTCR).

[5] This rule was changed in 1993 by a right-wing government but largely restored in 1998 after the left came to power.

this national bigamy, even going so far as using it as a kind of natural right, as Algerian President Abdelaziz Bouteflika did when he visited France in June 2000.

This pragmatic approach Algerians have towards French nationality influences the attitude of the other North African immigrant groups and, more broadly, all Muslim immigrants, placing them very far from Renan's ideal of an ongoing plebiscite. Some of them take a traditional individualist approach if they have enough material and cultural resources to back it up. But for most, Islam serves as a reassuring shared identity. You can become French because you stay loyal to your roots by visibly asserting your identity as a Muslim. Seen this way, the demand for institutionalisation, for creating a kind of 'local citizenship' tied to Islam, seems to spring from an integration policy that has played down and marginalized nationality, probably with some regret, and transferred the solemnity of it to Islam.

It is the reverse of the colonial system, in that being a recognised cultural minority may lead to special citizenship rights. This is alien to the entire spirit of Republicanism, which however cannot legitimately reject it unless it offers the prospect of a social mobility as good as that provided by a quota system run by groups that will quickly learn (if they have not already done so) how to trade their votes at election time for jobs and social security benefits, though these are probably easier to get locally and regionally than at national level.

But since France's system of producing its elites is based against the immigrant newcomers, other measures will probably be urgently needed, such as encouraging community activity, quietly giving preference to various groups and practising an unofficial positive discrimination already seen in sectors where there is ethnic conflict. A sort of reverse colonial system, with the equivalent of indigenous affairs administrators in charge of policy in cities and suburbs, keeping social order with doses of targeted aid and with grassroots bosses to apply the policies. This is perhaps an exaggeration, since nobody is cooking up such a system in France, but faced with the trouble created by youth violence, social systems tend to unthinkingly reproduce old patterns in new situations. Debate about the place of religion in the public arena or in education and about the icons of secularism and multiculturalism reflects a broad trend towards giving more weight to collective integration than to links between state and individual in building a national community.

The countries of southern Europe are still largely untouched by the social fallout from the changes that have been going on in the old northern industrial states for several decades, changes that were set off by the flow of immigrants from the south starting in the 1960s. They see the problem now as one of accepting permanent immigrants, whose religious culture too has to be incorporated into a new European identity. So the core of the negotiations is building a plural Europe that collectively embraces Islam and its culture and traditions and no longer requires just a prior individual written promise to obey the rules relative to other groups and needs. The aim is to establish a legitimate and visible presence with a strong identity. The notion of a useful invisibility steps up moderate pressure for recognition as a community. Solidarity with the outside is then only one aspect of settlement, which is concerned to share universal values while retaining a self-awareness based on Islam. This is shown by the importance of the mosques, which have taken over from political parties and trade unions, and whose faithful are identifiable by their clothing and food habits. There are some parallels here and there between the disavowal of violent manifestations of Islam and condemnation of old forms of secularism (though some groups and elites still cling to them). It can even make acceptance of a consensus conditional on renegotiation of the secular pact. This approach implies that the theoretical legitimacy of the state will only be recognised when the contractual framework of a new pluralism is in place and taking into account the values and solidarities of a group involved in a transition but concerned to recognise the everyday legitimacy of the state. This is like the situation of the French working class in the 1950s and the strategy of the communist party.

Success involves negotiating at various levels. The partner in France has long been the state, the focus of all symbolic representation and allegiances. It remains the key partner, the defender and provider of resources, but is not fully responding to change, especially to challenges to the institutions that underpin its legitimacy. The result of a shared but non-global strategy by North African immigrant elites is peaceful community organisation. Rivalry between individuals and groups, failed policies imposed by top levels of government that are sympathetic to group progress or advantage and that stabilise the group have delayed its growth.

This approach ultimately involves retaining ties with the state that avoid outbreaks of violence, while building an external arbitration link that can remove obstacles to collective recognition and broadening the relationship with local authorities and civil society. This is probably the most important change that has occurred since 1985. The elites are now investing most at local level, in businesses and in a social strategy involving mayors and state, religious, administrative and community partners who make local affairs a focus of their activity. An obsession with address-books remains an important feature of the elites and community groups and expands their contacts. But a new concern for professionalism and efficiency aims for success that is an example to others, especially in northern Europe but also in Spain and Italy. So the focus on local investment involves a dose of attention to the community amid still quite varied responses, including at individual level.

The debate is different in the south because immigration there is more recent and less family-based. The absorption of illegal immigrants from the southern and eastern Mediterranean is also part of an advantage in agricultural or industrial production that southern European countries retain over northern members of the European Union. This economic approach goes with an ideological rejection, based on the supposed incompatibility of Islam with national values, that is found in various forms in Italy, Spain and Greece, where immigrants from South America, Eastern Europe or the Philippines are preferred to those from Turkey, Albania or North Africa.

Some political players can thereby inject elements of older issues into the national debate, clearly taking it beyond national borders and perhaps creating a need for regulation on grounds of both human rights and egalitarian principles.

Politically and legally implementing a European citizenship that involves absorbing new immigrants is only just beginning. Sometimes it makes progress, including in southern Europe, thanks to a kind of transnational community of immigration experts, including researchers, officials, politicians and sometimes judges and police who handle such matters. Their exchanges and informal contacts shape law and administrative practice concerning nationality, citizenship, asylum and visas and anticipate policy questions.

So Europe is called upon to collectively manage new kinds of mobility found both in older host countries like France, where institutions handling immigration seem out of touch with the new situation, both at local and European level, in the countries that once produced immigrants and then became host countries themselves in the late 1980s and early 1990s (Italy, Spain, Portugal and Greece). Everywhere the foreigners make up a multi-hued patchwork, settling into corners of a segmented labour market, sometimes as illegals, often complementing the national workforce, and usually because of their lack of documents, which is mitigated by periodic regularization campaigns that are based more on length of residence than, as in the past (France 1981-82), on having a steady job. New forms of activism have sprung up alongside them, anticipating a constantly-changing citizenship whose restrictions are contested by those involved, who assert themselves through action. The quest for legal status by asylum-seekers (and the *Aussiedler* in Germany) is part of this approach.

These recent trends, where immigration has called into question old ideas of citizenship,[6] are what we have tried to highlight in this book. They are sometimes patched together and contradictory. The assertion of an Islamic identity that emerged as a basis of discussion and broadly of integration in the 1980s can lead just as much to multiculturalism as it can to communities shut away in new ghettos that defy the society outside and link up to international networks promoting various forms of violence. Others, sometimes from the same region but associated with immigrants from more distant parts, talk of globalisation and the free movement of people to create all-embracing social movements. They seek a common language to bring together Senegalese and Chinese but they turn to their advantage the mood of the times.

The two approaches conflict in various European countries with longer-established groups and spark minority reactions that feed the growth of the far right, as in Austria, Germany, Italy and France. Some see Europe's largely Christian culture, only recently opened up to Judaism, as being threatened by an Islam they know only through imported stereotypes. Other see the social systems and the welfare state, built after World War II, as threatened by unrestricted immigration. These defensive reactions cut across the old right-left divisions and come together, along with new fears raised by the enlargement of the European Union and the growth of regional awareness.

Immigration seen as part of a constant internal renewal of the European fabric, that the demographic crisis will help turn into a necessary/inevitable threat,

[6] C. Wihtol de Wenden and R. Leveau, *La Beurgeoisie. Les trois âges de la vie associative issue de l'immigration,* Paris, CNRS Editions, 2001.

is probably the biggest collective challenge to a European system that does not want to see itself as an infinitely-expanding empire, but which must open up to new areas, new cultures and the population movements that go with them if it wants to retain its influence and legitimacy.

Chapter 1

Research on Immigration, Islam and Citizenship in Western Europe: How Far Has a Specific Transdisciplinary Domain Been Established?

Vassoodeven Vuddamalay

Introduction

Research concerning immigration, Islam and citizenship issues has today attained a critical point. The situation has become excessively complex for organizations, social milieux and especially political elites questioned by such issues. Transnational scientific communities and funding-bureaucracies are called to understand the process of knowledge-accumulation in such fields, constantly interacting with international and national events. Research-chronologies show an almost similar pattern for almost all the major European countries, in the transition from the late 1970s' essentially socio-economic approach of migration to the 1990s' dominantly political and socio-religious approach. However, the new immigrant countries of Southern Europe are simultaneously having to deal with economic migrants, refugees and the emerging issue of Islam. The transformations of the European and national debates from purely economicist immigrant labour paradigms of the late 1970s and early 1980s, show how the specialised domains and their experts have come to acquire an overall dramatic[1] dimension. Specific

[1] The *tout Paris* feature illustrated by debates between French Islamologists, resulting in a special issue of the intellectual journal, *Esprit*, *A la recherche du monde musulman*, in July-September 2001 can ideally exemplify this evolution. This dossier was rediscussed in the pages of one of the Parisian intellectual institutions, that is the daily, *Le Monde*, in the issue of the 12 October 2001, by its religion specialist, H. Tincq. It seems that the French Islamologists have, to some extent, been responsible for the mediatization of the debates on islamism. The subtleties of French intellectual/ university life are here well illustrated, because it seems that there is a competition between sociologists and politologists on the one hand and then perhaps more vitally between the different researchers engaged in this field. H. Tincq reveals that G. Kepel, with the publication of his *Jihad, expansion et déclin de l'islamisme*, Gallimard, in spring 2000, has initiated some passionate debates in the

transdisciplinary domains on a European level are quickly emerging as immigration, Islam and citizenship research is being developed. Research teams have now become closely knit communities, not only on a national, European and/or Euro-American scale, but they are also increasingly linking with major non-Western states specialised with research-centres.

Within the fast increasing migration and Islam research and despite a growing europeanization of the debates, the national context has remained the dominant research framework. The institutional advancement towards a common political and economic space is to some extent blocked by strong national intellectual traits. The dominant national framework has resulted in distinct ways of accumulating knowledge in dominant national concepts, whereby the social scientists approach migration/Islam and the evolving issues. In fact, these national traits may to some extent hinder the identification of an essential missing link in migration and Islam debates, namely the impact of distinct European Orientalism(s). Orientalism as a specific scientific field has been left behind and more often forgotten by the intellectual and political elites until some events come to remind them of its usefulness. Hence, an understanding of the historical and socio-political background on the ways research has developed in the fields evoked above is now essential.

Research within these domains related to migration has become so stratified that, at times, it is remarked that the specialists themselves can sometimes forget the ever-necessary recontextualization of their specific researches within the more global European social sciences. Another important aspect is the re-introduction into the debates on a world-level of all the social sciences, and not only sociology or politics. Anthropology, geography and history which have helped more than other disciplines in reestablishing links with the wider domain of *Orientalism*, should be questioned in their interactions with migration, Islam and citizenship. However, in France the political sciences have built some early links with segments of the Orientalist institutions, resulting in the learning of Arab and other Oriental languages by the political scientists and also working-arrangements with the religious sciences, during the speeding up of the Islam debates as from the early 1980s. For instance, the French Ministry of Foreign Affairs through its research-institutes in the Muslim world[2] is close to the university-milieux specialised in the diverse countries which are today being investigated by the young French doctoral students. And, the post of the 'cadre d'Orient,' of the Ministry has traditionally attracted young politologists and students from the INALCO. Some observers will even remark that for several generations, some of these qualifications and socio-professional trajectories (often as diplomats) have been essentially coopted within the French/European aristocratic social milieux.

intelligentsia of Paris and within the main representative groups of the French provincial elites.

[2] See the contribution of O. Roy, 'Les islamologues ont-ils inventé l'islamisme?', to the special issue of the journal, *Esprit, A la recherche du monde musulman*, July-September 2001.

Furthermore, the impact on citizenship-research has resulted in a continuing reappraisal of the notion of citizenship, whereby the post-1945 American hegemony and the consequent americanization of European social theories have been postulated. We conclude with the debates concerning the role of the US as a looking-glass for European research in migration/Islam and citizenship issues. What are the new perspectives? What can be the future of the inter-European and Euro-American social scientific partnerships? Is the American dominance in these research-domains really challenged by the rich diversity of the European approaches? Concerning the specific dimensions of the American dominance on European Sociology,[3] some specialists in the post-1989 events, have been introducing the debates concerning these specific Euro-American relations in the domain of social scientific researches. In 1998, the British scholar, Adrian Favell has also been pursuing a long-term work on the consequences of American researches on Europe in the specific areas of immigration, integration and citizenship issues.

Migration and Islam research in post-1945 Europe: How to recontextualize these new research-fields?

European social sciences have been heavily marked by the two world wars. The First World War has been witnessing the end of the institutionalization-process of most Western European sociologies, often in close interactions with American sociology. During the interwar years, this process was materialised by the setting-up of social scientific research-centres and the rise of specific schools of thought. However, this movement has been interrupted by the imminence of the Second World War. Research-institutions established in most of the European states have been transformed from their initial objectives through the exile of their distinguished researchers. The Frankfurt School[4] (1923-1950) has been one of the most illustrious examples of that period. Robert Park inversely seen as one of the founders of the Chicago Urban Sociology and of the mode of ethnic monographs relied also on European thinkers. Post-1945 social sciences have been generalised throughout Europe and specific schools of thought and sub-disciplines[5] have gone through a massive development in accordance with particular national political and

[3] See L. Scaff, in a contribution, '*Europe and America in Search of sociology : Reflections on a Partnership*', in B. Nedelmann and P. Sztompka (Eds.), *Sociology in Europe. In Search of Identity*, Walter de Gruyter, Berlin, 1993, Berlin ; A. Favell, *Philosophies of Integration. Immigration and the Idea of Citizenship in France and Britain*, 2nd Edition, Palgrave Publishers Ltd, in association with Centre for Research in Ethnic Relations, University of Warwick, 2001.

[4] *Cf.* M. Jay, *The Dialectical Imagination*, Little Brown & Company, Boston, 1973 and was then first translated in 1977 and then in 1989 at the Editions Payot, Paris, *L'Imagination dialectique. L'école de Francfort, 1923-1950.*

[5] Such as it has been the case with the *Sociology of work* in France, which to some extent, from its initial dominantly marxist standpoint has been the starting-point of migration-research and the increase in the specialised literature.

scientific systems. Migration and Islam research is still institutionally an underdeveloped sector within most social sciences and attempts are made to understand its institutional weaknesses despite a massive growth of field-research, which is quite generously funded by national, supranational specialised organizations and by private foundations. A chronology of global migration and Islam research will contribute to this tentative understanding.

Migration and Islam research in Europe has emerged as specific research-domains only during the past 15 to 20 years. These domains are today marked by a fast-increasing rate of publication. The language-factor and the diverse scientific cultures add to the already existent difficulties to synthetize and classify these publications. Despite increasing programs built within an inter-European, Euro-American or even Euro-Australian scales, research-teams and individual researchers have largely carried out their work within a *national framework approach*. Even then, this national boundedness of migration and Islam-research should be recontextualized within the post-1945 changes brought about in European social sciences.[6] How have these issues of migration, the institutionalization of Islam in European countries and the changing definitions of integration/citizenship been influencing the diverse disciplines within the University?

Recording and classifying fast-increasing researches in these highly politicised domains as migration and Islam on a European scale is today a major challenge. Is it academically pertinent to record and discuss all the works that are continually being published on these issues? Or rather should not a regular assessment or state-of-the-art be seen as a pre-requisite work in these fast-advancing research-fields? The political elites and the national and supranational bureaucracies who usually fund these research-activities have much to gain through such interactions with the scientific communities. What methodologies can then be set up in order to be able to account synthetically for the growing diversity of actors who intervene on societal/ political issues? Researchers are increasingly being solicited by the medias and the political classes and their main activities are hence being carried out within the States or the European Commissions' policy-oriented needs.

How will it be possible to identify the main schools of thought, research-teams or even individual researchers and discuss their work? Researchers and teams who have been working on almost the same *problematiques* during the past two decades or so and have been publishing in specialised journals are discussed here. However, these more recent works of the past 20 to 30 years should be reexamined within a more long-term framework. This may allow us to understand

[6] B. Nedelmann and P Sztompka (eds.), *Sociology in Europe. In Search of Identity*, de Gruyter, Berlin, 1993; F. Ringer, *Fields of Knowledge. French Academic Culture in Comparative Perspective, 1890-1920*, Cambridge University Press/Editions de la Maison des Sciences de l'Homme, Cambridge, 1992; Ch. C. Lemert, (ed.), *French Sociology: Rupture and Renewal Since 1968*, New York, Columbia University Press, 1981; W. Lepenies, *Between Literature and Science. The Rise of Sociology*, Cambridge University Press, Cambridge, 1985.

how far this ever-specialised domain of migration, Islam and citizenship research is increasingly influencing social theory. Some of the younger and more Europeanist sociologists, are today exploring these new avenues of research and are trying to add more impetus to their work in a comparatist European approach within a Euro-American context.[7] To some extent, migration-research should be recontextualised within a long-term understanding of the scientific and political background of the development of the social sciences both on Euro-American and inter-European levels.

Chronological development of migration and Islam research as from the mid-1970s: The identification of four sub-periods

Migration and Islam-research is tentatively divided into four sub-periods, a chronology which has been more or less observed in most European countries. France is taken as one of the meaningful sites of approach as we have been working on this specific political and scientific context for the past 15 years. The French case is necessarily compared to other European scientific contexts. These sub-periods are listed below and discussions are held within the larger frameworks of post-1945 European social sciences.

The first period (1970/74 to 1981/82), shows us the first collective works done by French social scientists mainly in Paris. The *Centre d'études sociologiques* of rue Cardinet,[8] transferred during the 1980s to the IRESCO of rue Pouchet was the meeting-point of these pioneering French researchers.

The second sub-period (1981-1989), is marked by two major events during the same decade *within the European landscape*. The political protest Marches of the Beurs[9] in the early eighties were succeeded by the emergence of Islam in the public French/British spheres with the Creil Headscarf and Rushdie Affairs. The research-teams began then to specialise themselves, giving rise to local research-centres in the main provincial university cities, which tend to oppose themselves to the '*tout Paris*' mentality.[10]

[7] *Cf.* A. Favell's revisiting some American researchers' work concerning the European states or M. Bommes' project to study migration within a Luhmannite and Parsonian approach.

[8] One working-paper in 1976 informs us about the pioneering researchers, who gathered within the Equipe de recherches sur l'immigration - CNRS. This pluridisciplinary team which will have a very short life, published their first synthesis, *Recherches sur l'immigration*, in January-March 1976, within the framework of the, *Société des Amis du Centre d'études sociologiques*, 82, rue Cardinet, 75017 Paris.

[9] See a major synthesis of the Beur political movements in France, in C. Withol de Wenden and R. Leveau, *La Beurgeoisie. Les trois âges de la vie associative issue de l'immigration*, CNRS éditions, mai 2001, Paris.

[10] See the work of Ch. C. Lemert, who discusses about this specific Parisian feature of a dense intellectual life and the consequent competition for public attention, which he called the *tout Paris* feature, in, *French Sociology. Rupture...*, *op. cit.* and also his articles, ' Literary Politics and the Champ of French Sociology,' *Theory and Society*, 1981, vol. 10,

The third period (1989-1996), results in the generalization of doctoral researches on a European scale and the emergence of a second and/or third generation of researchers who will increasingly meet their European and American university colleagues.

And the last period (1996-2000), has seen the publication of these doctoral dissertations and also of growing cross-national colloquys.

However, within post-1945 European social sciences, migration and Islam research has been progressing quite unevenly. Despite the quite early problems caused by large-scale immigration of Muslim foreign workers, migration and Islam-research and their impact on the citizenship issue have only been able to emerge as a *fin-de-siècle* feature within European social sciences. Scholars in the different states have been making their own national assessments as from the late 1980s and during the 1990s. Some specialised journals have been developed since the late 1970s or early 1980s and some with a more pronounced European dimension appeared during the 1990s. Transatlantic research-traditions in the areas of immigration, interracial or interethnic problems have also been developed at an early stage. However, the Americans have sometimes preceded their European colleagues in these emerging research and political domains. Gary Freeman, Mark Miller, Aristide Zolberg, Martin Schain and many others have been working on these issues before the massive entry of the European social scientists in the ever-increasing debates. What periodization can be set up? How to account for the specific geography of the European migration and Islam-research? How can we link the socio-spatial expansion of these research-domains to their specific chronology?

What can be the phases within a global European chronology? Establishing within a 30 to 50 years' period a meaningful chronology of migration/Islam research requires a preliminary knowledge of historical turning-points corresponding in the political field, to specific symbolical events. The immediate post Second World War does not correspond to any significant event, until the early 1970s. *The Thirty Glorious Years (1945-1975)* were primarily seen as a period during which the migration-process was restricted to purely economic and manpower needs in the industrial reconstruction of post-Second World War Europe. The typical immigrant was a single working-class man, who, having left his family behind, was mostly involved in the sending country's political struggles. His cultural and religious identity was not seen as an essential factor in his individual and collective behaviour. Much emphasis was laid on industrial strikes and class conflicts. Significant geographical and socio-economic researches were made and an initial accumulation of knowledge in the social sciences concerned with migration was then made. These socio-economic researches were then

n°5, pp. 645-669 and also, 'French Sociology: After the Patrons, What?,' *Contemporary Sociology*, 1986, vol. 15, n°5, pp. 689-692. Concerning this specific trait as to the intricacies of the French (usually Parisian) University and the links with a wider readership, see the dossier of *Esprit* in the summer 2001, *A la recherche du monde musulman,* where some specialists as Burgat, Roussillon and Roy have discussed some of the shortcomings of French Islam-research.

preeminent and did contribute to the ignoring of other quite fundamental[11] scientific activities.

The recession years (1975-1995)

Following the oil-crisis of the early 1970s and resulting unemployment, most European states started to put an end to massive labour migration. In July 1974, the government of Jacques Chirac decided to halt the massive entries of foreign workers. Economic crisis added to the dramatising of emerging political debates, in the wake of the racist disorders in Marseilles in 1973. After the Marcellin-Fontanet circular (1972) which refused to regularize illegals, the cessation of labour migration in July 1974 had many unexpected consequences. Large-scale family reunion, the intensification of illegal immigration due to the strong pull factors in the recruiting sectors (as the building sector, domestic services, clothing industry, restaurant and catering services) and the shift from industrial to political and socio-religious issues were among some of these societal repercussions.

However, within the 1975-1995 period, some meaningful political events occurred, which were seemingly outside the predicting aptitudes of most experts. From the cessation of the large-scale labour migration to the massive settlement of migrant communities within each of the European country, the entry of the second generations into the political systems and especially the religious visibility of Muslim minorities in urban Europe have been heralding these radical changes which are today taking place in that continent. As from the early 1980s, political analyses of the migrant minorities in Europe started to increase, until the sudden emergence of Islam as a second or third religion within these European states. Such changes are now included in the scientific communities' agenda and also by specific departments of different Ministries. The European Commissions and the American-German-Italian-British Foundations have been increasing researches into these political issues, especially after the threats posed by radical Muslim groups throughout the world and especially within segments of the migrant communities in Europe and North America.

The politics of Space in European migration and Islam research: The Dominant National Analytical Framework

A review of the European states' specific migration-research shows the dominance of the national framework approach. We will proceed with the study of some specific states, namely the 'core-countries' which have been receiving the largest migrant communities and also the largest Muslim components. Then the medium-

[11] Such as the largely unknown publications of specialists coming from the CHEAM for R. Montagne in the late 1950s and Orientalist institutions as the *Langues O* for L. Massignon, the Lieutenant-Colonel Justinard by the late 1920s in such publications as the *Revue d'études islamiques/musulmanes*.

sized and/or less central countries will be dealt with. The core-countries seem to be more nationalistic, whilst the small or medium-sized ones seem to be more Europeanist in their approaches. To some extent, the most innovative research-works have appeared in the smaller countries, such as can be testified by the pioneering research on Islam as a European political issue. For instance, the Louvain sociologists have preceded the other main research-clusters, such as the Parisian politologists, on account of the specific national contexts and also because locally the sociology of religion was solidly established. The French jacobinist model can be compared to the other European decentralised university and research-systems. German and British decentralised Orientalist institutions have been more dynamic than French Orientalism in migration and Islam research.

Apart from establishing an elementary chronology of the different research-works concerned with immigration/Islam and citizenship issues in Europe, their geographical diversity and range provide a first tentative system through which a more minute classification (leading us to a system of sub-categories) can be set up. It is obvious that the national framework has been the dominant one. The Western European social scientists have not themselves, (until the early-1990s) been doing comparatist research-works on such issues as migration/Islam (namely its acceptance as another extraneous non-Western religion) and citizenship (questioned moreover through its globalization paradigm). Despite the generalization of some collective research-works on these issues always bearing the titles of, *Islam(s) in Europe* or *Immigration/citizenship/integration in Europe*, each single state is more or less studied by its own specialists. However, some of the younger migration-specialists are increasingly becoming Europeanist in their range and styles of work, moving through the distinct political and social scientific geographies of the Western states. Some of them move quite easily within the distinct social sciences and concepts which are commonly used by the distinct national researchers coming from the different European states.

A European geography of migration and Islam research-activities: What have been their modes of circulation?

The geographical distribution of the European migration and Islam research-work and its specific modes of circulation should today be more regularly evaluated by the social scientific milieux. These assessments should contribute to improving research itself and also to responding to ever-growing demands coming from diverse spheres of the European/Western world. The chronologies established for some of the European states are well known by the younger and more Europeanist researchers. However, after some thirty years of active research, the factors influencing the spatial distribution of migration and Islam research and their consequences on the circulation of knowledge are still not properly studied. Is it still too early to examine the impact and role of such specialised domains within the broader social sciences and more so, their impact on the construction of social theory?

The spatialization of research-activities shows how some cities and their specialised scientific communities and research-centres have become major places of inter-European and Euro-American scientific meetings. In fact, in the early days of migration-research, within the distinct European states, working-traditions have been established between the specialised expert groups, the decisional milieux within the higher spheres of the administration of the states, the ruling groups of the associations. These habits set up within a national context, have been quite rapidly changed by the rising europeanizing trends taking place as from the late 1980s and during the 1990s. According to some specialists, the dominant national paradigms will in the context of increasing supranational trends in research, be replaced by an underlying regionalist discourse. However, is it not too early to anticipate for the whole of Europe what still appears only as a tentative approach within some specific states, which have inherited from decentralist and regionalist traditions in their intellectual and political debates?

As soon as the first national research-works (more usually, the doctoral dissertations) have been published as from the mid-1980s, the different researchers and research-teams or centres began to approach the European problematiques and its specific geopolitical, socio-cultural and economical dimensions, the national paradigms began to lose strength vis-à-vis the complex interrelations between seemingly Muslim – dominated immigrant settlements and European political systems. Consequently, the other religious faiths have been sometimes forgotten or rather underestimated during the speeding up of research on migration and more specifically the Islam issue. Hence, the sudden increase of Islam-research has changed the established traditions in most of the social sciences of religion, which tend to be less hermetic and more open to the other social sciences. The rapid politicization of islamic issues in most Western societies, on account of the evolution of the post-Cold War international relations has undoubtedly resulted in excessive funding of research in order to be able to respond to their security needs.

The French specificities

The specific French migration and Islam research has revealed itself to be still heavily centralised on Paris and its most elitist networks. Apart from a pre-history of a really pluridisciplinary migration work within the *Centre d'études sociologiques* on Cardinet street in the 17th Parisian district, and the consequent decentralization within some of the big cities in the provinces, the speeding up of research-work has caused the competition to make a comeback to Paris, which is still and will remain for long the nerve-centre of France. The politologists have more than in the other European states been at the start and sudden acceleration of Islam-research and in its introduction in teaching in the doctoral units at the IEP (Paris and Aix-Marseille) and also indirectly determinant in the EHESS (Paris and Marseille). The traditional typical power-struggles between the sociological and politological institutions have been perpetuated. A research-work on these conflicts will help in understanding the factors underlying these conflictual situations, especially for foreign specialists coming to work in France. Most of the provincial units working on migration have, in fact, been developing strong traditions which are undoubtedly linked to their pioneering researchers (in accordance with the patterns set up by the patrons and prophets), their local/regional specificities, and the customs and habits which have been in practice for years. We will try to understand comparatively with other European states, the strong centralist French traditions. How is it that some of its best research-units are still localised in Paris and especially those concerned with classical social sciences as sociology and anthropology, and also those related to the less known Orientalist institutions? How far have its political sciences been able to develop working-relations with the Orientalist traditions and also with the specific sociology of religions?

The British and German contexts

Britain and Germany seem to converge in the social scientific and geographical organization of research. Their decentralised model corresponds to the political organization of their space. Their best research-centres are localised outside their capital-cities. These decentralised research-works have yet to be assessed for a wider European readership, especially for Germany, where the language-barrier seems to have a great influence. Increasing university collaborations between the Parisian politologists and German Islam specialists, through the ***Marc Bloch Centre*** of Berlin in the early and mid-1990s seem to have resulted in the growth of comparatist discourses. Should this rising Franco-German comparatist trend be seen as detrimental to Franco-British cooperation?

From a disciplinary approach, British researches have been quite early mobilising across a vast array ranging from anthropology/sociology, the educational sciences whilst in France, the politists have been and are still at the forefront of this new research-domain. Before the Rushdie Affair, Islam was primarily seen in Britain as part of the entire Muslim culture, whilst the French from the start have been studying the Islam of the immigrant populations through their political aspects. Britain sees itself as a political exception for the whole of the European continent, namely because of its insular situation, its political and especially its colonial history, the planetary expansion of its language which is becoming the medium of exchanges between the Europeans. Jorgen Nielsen has been the first or among the first, in 1992, to publish a work embracing the whole European continent, ***Muslims in Western Europe*** (Edinburgh University Press). He then published in 1997, ***The Christian-Muslim Frontier*** (Taurus Editions, London) and in 1999, ***Towards a European Islam***, (Macmillan Press, London, in association with the Centre for Research in Ethnic Relations, University of Warwick). Despite their insular geographical position, the British will to some extent, open up their research-activities to the whole of Europe.

The other social scientist, who has experienced a rapid European dimension is Steven Vertovec after his training in the American universities of Colorado and California. He is initially known for his work on the Hindu populations in the former British colony of Trinidad, (***Hindu Trinidad. Religion, ethnicity and socio-Economic Change***), then for his direction at the sides of Ceri Peach and Colin Clarke, of, ***South Asians Overseas***: ***Migration and Ethnicity***,

Cambridge 1990; and the more recent, *Islam in Europe and The Politics of Religion and Community*, Macmillan, Basingstoke, 1997. The other rising social scientist in the British context is Danièle Joly, author in 1994 of, *British Crescent. Making a Place for Muslims in British society*, (Avebury, Aldershot). She has also participated in the collective work, *Muslims in Britain. An annotated Bibliography 1960-1984. Bibliographies in Ethnic Relations*, n°4, 1985. She is today the Director of the centre for Research in ethnic Relations (CRER of Warwick University). She is now working on the refugees issue in Europe. These scientific milieux concentrated at the start in the Midlands (rather than in London and its suburbs) are now extending to the whole of Britain, with the coming of specialists of international Relations from the Universities of Durham, Lancaster and Exeter. Another feature of British research is the relatively important community emerging from the ethnic minorities,[12] which is probably weaker than in Germany but certainly stronger than in France.

In Germany research initiatives have been numerous, but they seem to be dispersed between the diverse universities and their specialised centres. No single school of thought has emerged, such as it has been the case with the French IEP's networks. The German researchers are geographically dispersed between the universities and distinct disciplines. The main centres of Islam-research are the following: Turkish Studies and Sociology in the Universities of Essen and Bamberg, International Relations in the University of Georg-August of Gottingen, the Orient Intitute of Hamburg, the Centre of documentation on the Islamo-Christian Relations (CIBEDO) of Frankfurt, Islamology and Orientalism of the Centre of the Modern Orient of Berlin.[13] Would these initiatives result in a form of dispersion and also in the absence of more synthetical work, which have been published in the other Central and Northern European countries?

Some non-German research-units, namely the French politologists have tried to start some comparatist works as from the late 1980s until the mid-1990s. In fact, the first cluster around the CERI, namely the specialist of the Kurdish issue, Hamit Bozarslan and Riva Kastoryano have as from the early1980s started their comparatist approaches of Turkish immigrants in France and Germany. Rémy Leveau in 1998 in, 'Islam : laïcité à la française et modèle pluraliste allemand' has attempted to contextualize his venue at the *Marc Bloch Institute* of Berlin in a comparatist approach of French political sociology and German Orientalism. This Franco-German venture of the 1990s has been materialised by doctoral dissertations, colloquys and their systematic publications. The language-barrier, can in the case of the German language hinder the circulation of German research-works. Furthermore, the strong influence of Orientalist traditions in German Islam-research would also have contributed to its being hermetic for German non-

[12] See for instance, the work of T. Modood, 'British Asian Muslims and the Rushdie Affair,' *British Political Quarterly*, n°61, 1990; 'Ethno-religious minorities, secularism and the British State' , *British Political Quarterly*, n°65, 1994.

[13] The following researchers are present in these institutions, Yasemin Karakasoglu, Lale Yalçin-Heckmann, Bassam Tibi, Hans Vocking and Gerdien Jonker. The work of Werner Ruf at the University of Kassel should also be included.

specialists. Paradoxically, the German University has had less difficulty than the French research-institutions to reintroduce the Orientalist know-how and specialised knowledge of the Muslim groups in Germany/Europe in today's Islam debates in the West. To some extent, Orientalists have been opposed to the more classical social scientists, as politists and sociologists in the speeding up of the Islam-issues in the German public space.

The other European countries

Southern Europe, the Netherlands, Belgium have been gathered together as they possess some similar traits in the specific European context, despite some substantial differences between them. One of their main characteristics is the fact that these secondary countries seem to be less nationalistic in their approaches of the migration, Islam and citizenship issues. When replaced in the wider European context, these issues are traditionally examined within a more dispassionate framework by these medium-sized countries. They have been producing more comparatist works, as they have been used through their political history to be plurilingual, pluricultural and to practise a more active European allegiance.

Southern Europe has emerged as a new immigrant space only within the last 15-20 years. Migration and Islam research has been developed as distinct scientific domains only within a decade. However, the two main immigrant countries show some specificities, in that immigration and Islam are becoming major political and societal issues. University-research has, to some extent, been dependent at least, at its beginning, on other sectors, namely the Christian Churches' organizations. In Italy, the more recent specialists such as Stefano Allievi, M. Boormans, Chantal Saint-Blancat and Ottavia Schmidt di Friedberg have been pursuing their higher and more specialised training in other European countries. With more than half-a-million Muslims, Italy is today having to deal institutionally and scientifically with Islam as a public issue.[14] Moreover, Stefano Allievi and Felice Dassetto have observed (1993), that '*the Ambroisian Islam (that is, Milanese) appears to be so much integrated in the local environment that it intersects with the deep prejudices of the ordinary Milanese against Rome.*' Would Milanese and Turinian Islam be better integrated to their local urban geography and politics than that of Rome in the traditional Italian conflicts opposing the industrial North and the political Centre? Furthermore, the role of the Vatican in the establishment of some Christian-Muslim initiatives has been ignored by the researchers. Jorgen Nielsen has described in 1999 the importance of the Christian religious institutions in the new immigrant countries. The same pattern concerning the pioneering role of the Churches in the accumulation of knowledge which has been observed in the core-countries is reproduced in Southern Europe. Until the early 1990s, the Churches' personalities have quite often been the Southern

[14] O. Schmidt di Friedberg, 'Stratégies des migrants et positionnement de l'islam en Italie,' *in* R. Leveau (dir.), *Islam(s) en Europe*, *op. cit.*

European's representatives in the Islam debates concerning their respective countries.

In Spain, the contribution asked from Father Antonio Rodriguez, the Delegate of the Diocese of Madrid to the foreigners in the special issue of the Parisian journal, *Projet*, as late as 1992 is quite significant. The social scientists emerging only in the mid-1990s will indicate the initial state of their researches concerning the immigrants and more so, concerning the more sensitive issue of Islam. Historically, Southern Europe has been through their geography, the first part of Western Europe to be affected by the settlement of substantial Muslim communites. However, the Muslim presence of the 5th extending until the 11th Century in the Sultanate of Sicily and the more reputed *Dar el Islam* of Andalusia from the 9th to the 14th Century was politically different from that of today's dominantly immigrant working classes. Some of the former representations are still present in today's political debates. Bernabé López García,[15] in his current researches in the Spanish context seems to answer to some of these queries. These issues are pertinent today as some of the European social scientists seem to refer to the huntingtonian division of the world into fundamentally antagonistic cultural and socio-religious areas. The geopolitical importance of Southern Europe, which is more affected by the new refugees and migratory movements in the Balkans and the Maghreb/Machrek can here be emphasized.

Would the Southern European countries suffer from an anteriority or rather inferiority complex vis-à-vis the core French, British and German important scientific and political experience? Some of the Southern European researchers would underline these aspects in the literature-reviews, usually introducing their own researches. Maribel Fierro and Maria-Jesus Carnicero have coordinated a field-research, 'La communauté musulmane espagnole', from September 1993 until August 1994 and the work was funded by the *Instituto de Cooperacion con el Mundo Arabe*. Jordi Moreras, trained as a cultural anthropologist of Euro-Arab Studies and as a Coordinator of migration-research at the Foundation CIDOB,[16] published a monograph, *Musulmanes en Barcelona. espacios y dinamicas comunitarias* (CIDOB edicions). Field-researches are more frequent and a distinct Islam and migration domain is emerging. However, until recently the same specialists[17] have been present in the diverse colloquys, seminars and other

[15] One of the research-reports of B. López García has the following significant sub-title, 'Le retour des Maures', 'Immigración maghrebi en Espana. El retorno de los moriscos,' Madrid, 1993. Other researches have also been done such as, M. García-Arenal, ' El problema morisco : enfoques y cuestiones que pueden ser utiles para la situacion actual' and M. J. Viguera, 'Al-Andalus como interferencia,' which were read at the International Symposium, ' Comunidadaes islamicas en Espana y an la Comunidad Europea,' *El Escorial*, 2-5 March 1993.

[16] Barcelone's Centre of Information and International Documentation.

[17] S. Allievi and O. Schmidt di Friedberg for Italy and for Spain, M. Fierro, Montserrat A., A. Izquierdo Escribano from the Madrid University Computense, B. López García, and the representative of the Madrid Diocese to the foreign communities, A. Martinez Rodrigo have quite often been describing for an extra-Spanish readership the situation concerning the migration and Islam issues.

international actions of communications. These countries are however fast diversifying their university-courses and the younger generations of researchers are now present in their specialised centres. The cleavages between the Orientalist and theological approches and their classical social sciences which were identified in the core-countries are also reproduced in such countries as Italy. For instance, the Vatican institutions and its impact in the religious and social sciences through the *Institut pontifical d'études arabes et islamistiques* (Pisai) and its journal, *Islamochristiana* and especially its *Conseil pontifical pour le dialogue interreligieux* should be reassessed in today's debates.

In the Netherlands, the two specialists, Wasif Shadid and S. Van Koeningsveld[18] are known on a European scale after their coordination of the communications of several researchers in autumn 1995. Specialists and doctoral students coming from the Free University of Amsterdam, the Catholic University of Nijmegen and the Leiden University have contributed to this project on a national Dutch level. Other specialists such as Nico Landmann, Thijl Sunier, Jan Rath, Jeroën Doomernik, Rinus Penninx have been also among the first European social scientists to publish on the Islam issue in such journals as the *Ethnic and Racial Studies* and the former *New Community*. Belgium has revealed itself to be quite specific in that Felice Dassetto in his Catholic University of Louvain has been able to develop Islam research on a European scale. *The Forum for Research on Islam in Europe* and the series, 'Musulmans d'Europe' within the Parisian publishing house, L'Harmattan, have been some of the more recent initiatives to develop Islam-research. The links set up between the Catholic University of Louvain and the research milieux on religion in Strasbourg are perhaps the first institutional steps in the Europeanization of Islam-research. Furthermore, contradictory debates within a national context are still the dominant aspects. Divergent schools of thought within a European scale are still exceptional. In fact, Felice Dassetto has perhaps been among the rare observers of the political and scientific debates to develop these necessary inter-European debates, in his (*Construction de l'islam européen. Une approche socio-anthropologique*, 1996 and more recently in his coordination, of, *Islamic Words. Individuals, societies and discourse in contemporary European Islam*, 2000).

[18] These two researchers have organised the meetings of European specialists of the Islam issue on the theme, 'Islam, Hinduism and Politics in Western Europe', Leiden, 7-9 September 1995. This meeting marked the end of a national project, 'Religions of Ethnic Groups in the Netherlands', which was funded by the *Foundation for Research in Philosophy and Theology*.

A missing link in migration and Islam research: The place of European orientalism(s)

Migration/Islam field research and orientalist scientific traditions

Orientalism as a research-tradition that can contribute to today's *societal issues pertaining to* Islam's entry in the public spheres of most Western countries, has yet to be properly studied. It still appears in the early 21st Century as an *emerging domain* vis-à-vis the new problems brought about by massive immigration from former European colonies, some of them composed of a majority Muslim population. French social scientists concerned about the Islam-issue made some passing remarks about the interrelations of the social sciences and Orientalism. And, French Orientalists have also tried to inform in 1993, in their *Livre Blanc de l'Orientalisme français*, the decisional milieux of the Ministry of Education about their importance in intercultural issues and about their roles as a specialised community to protect the cultural heritage of the immigrant populations. The Parisian politist Rémy Leveau in the late 1990s, for instance, made some tentative remarks within the broader comparatist context of French political sociology and German Orientalism. And, the sociologist Fanny Colonna has been questioning the weaknesses of the *French Sociology of religion* vis-à-vis a very lively Orientalist tradition, itself much influenced by India, China and other faraway countries (core-periphery relations). Lucette Valensi has been debating about the marginal place of the Maghreb and Islam in the making of Durkheimian sociology (1984). In the same work edited by Jean-Claude Vatin, Edmund Burke III introduced debates concerning Islam within the broader issue of French Orientalism.[19] In Britain and Germany, on the contrary, specialists of the Islam-issue in Europe seem to come from their Oriental institutes (SOAS of London or the Orient Institute of Hamburg). Researchers coming from these Institutes have developed their own particular ways of doing research on Islam in the West. But, what about the American scholar, Barbara Metcalf, present on many panels and who also has been meeting some distinct research networks? She has been one of the first to try a comparatist approach on Islam in North America and Europe (1996) and she has also been present as early as 1988/1989, in a South Asia Seminar at Pennsylvania University on the topic '*Orientalism and Beyond*'?

However, as an original approach in studying today's Islam in Europe, Orientalism has yet to be put to good use (at least, in France at the INALCO) in the new approaches needed to understand *transplanted* Islam. Olivier Roy[20] is

[19] In his, '*The First Crisis of Orientalism, 1890-1914*' (1984), almost 5 years after his contribution, '*The French Tradition of the Sociology of Islam*' to another collective work, *Islamic Studies. A Tradition and Its Transformation*, edited in Santa Monica, California at the Undena University Press by Malcolm Kerr (1980).

[20] See his pertinent analysis of the role of French politologists in the generalization of Islam-research, in his contribution, 'Les islamologues ont-ils inventé l'islamisme?,' to the specifically Parisian journal, *Esprit*, August-September 2001, Special Issue, *A la recherche du monde musulman*. These debates within the university community will rapidly cross the

perhaps one of the few exceptions. Partly trained at the INALCO and as a politologist at the Parisian IEP, he did one of his first fieldworks on Islam in Afghanistan, before starting to write on European Islam. To some extent, the Orientalists' experience, know-how and also theoretical knowledge acquired during the past *two to three centuries* in the former colonial *fields* have yet to be fully *put to use* in the new fields of Muslim suburban and ethnic quarters of European cities.[21] Recent fieldworks in the Parisian suburban town of Mantes-la-Jolie and other symbolic places in France/Europe, have shown how the rivalries opposing the different groups are based on clanic and regional allegiances. A preliminary knowledge of conflicts and power-management in the sending regions can help avoid the difficult conditions of fieldwork in such areas and on such aspects as the control of a local Mosque. However, on a more general level it is observed that non-european specialists are specific in the ways of dealing with Orientalism/Islam in Europe and elsewhere throughout the world. This can be accounted for by their fundamentally comparatist approaches. Their transatlantic trainings and their diverse fieldworks (such as Indian Islam for B.D. Metcalf [22] who did her first major work on the Deobandis) are some of these new and

porous frontiers existing between the University itself and the medias, such as they will be explained to an informed public, which is the daily readership of the newspaper, *Le Monde*, by its religion specialist, H. Tincq, 'Le post-islamisme, réalité ou vue de l'esprit'. Les catégories de la science politique occidentale sont-elles adaptées à l'étude du monde musulman? La revue, *Esprit*, ouvre ses colonnes à des islamologues divisés', *Le Monde*, Wednesday 12 September 2001. Reference should also be made to his major publications, as, *L'Afghanistan : islam et modernité politique*, Paris, Le Seuil, 1985 ; *L'Echec de l'islam politique*, Le Seuil, Paris, 1992 and also his more recent, 'Vers un islam européen,' *Esprit*, Paris, 1999.

[21] See the contribution of V. Vuddamalay, 'L'islam institutionnel et l'islam informel : le cas de Mantes-la-Jolie,' in *Les Nouveaux territoires de la citoyenneté en Europe*, Colloque Ford Foundation/IFRI, 18/01/2001, to be published in *Les Cahiers de l'IFRI*, Summer/Fall 2002. The Mosque was in fact, the first one to be built with the institutional acceptance of the local Municipality, at that time headed by a Socialist teacher, who was born in Algeria. It seems at the time of our fieldwork, that a form of Ourzazati Islam headed by an industrial worker of the local Renault firm of Flins, who has been leading a local Muslim association in the Yvelines during the past 25 years had the upperhand, despite some fierce opposition especially from the Muslim youth born in the neighborhood of Le Val Fourré, where the concentration of foreign populations reaches almost 80 per cent, among whom the Moroccans are the leading group. The maps of L. Massignon, of R. Montagne and those of Colonel Justinard in the late 1930' concerning the concentrations of Maghrebian groups (traditionally coming from the same clans, villages or *douars*) in Paris and its suburbs have been helpfull. The work of R. Leveau, (*Le Fellah marocain, défenseur du trône*, Presses de le FNSP, 1985), helps in understanding the rural organizations and especially their links with their local/regional Islams.

[22] B. D. Metcalf, *Islamic Revival in British India: Deoband, 1860-1900*, Princeton, 1982 and the more recent work she coordinated, *Making Muslim Space in North America and Europe*, University of California Press, 1996, Berkeley and Los Angeles. It should be reminded that the Talibans in Afghanistan and Pakistan seem to be inspired by the religious reforms of Indian Islam in the mid-19th Century, namely among these Deobandis.

sometimes quite old traditions of work (such as, Edmund Burke III on Morocco and French Orientalism in the Maghreb and the Middle-East).

Traditional social sciences and orientalism in the European countries

Power-struggles in most European countries oppose their Orientalist institutions[23] and their traditional social sciences departments in the Universities. These potentially conflictual relations have been manifesting themselves diversely in accordance with the institutions' distinct political and intellectual histories. In France, specialists from INALCO would disdain the sociologists and politologists for not being able to *master* the languages and not be more intimate with the cultures of the Muslim groups. Their approaches of 'Islam at home/*à domicile*' would be seen as being over-pragmatic, excessively politicised and especially of being over-dependent on the political/ administrative authorities' needs. Would not these critics meet the first remarks against the French politologists made by the Catholic University of Louvain's team around Felice Dassetto, who was, in fact, the first with Albert Bastenier, to publish a book on Islam within a European country, *L'islam transplanté*, (1984, EPO) and has been continuing to publish within increasingly European networks?[24] In Germany, on the contrary, Orientalists seem to be more visible than the sociologists/politologists. Some implicit rivalries would oppose the Orientalists to the more institutionalised research-centres specialised in migration. A quick survey of German Islam-research shows the prominence of the Orientalist Institutes set up in the University-towns of the different Länders. These German institutions can be compared especially to those located in France but less so in Britain and Northern/Southern Europe, where the Christian religious milieux have been playing an active rôle and have often been dynamic agents alongside *the European Orientalists*. Furthermore, in these same German Institutes, scholars originating from the Turkish minority groups seem to be dynamic. This ethnic minority's presence in the German Universities will inevitably have an important consequence on the research-productivity concerning immigration/Islam in the coming years.

Ethnic minority researchers' presence in the different European countries should by now become an important issue, as the minorities' influences in the economic and political fields are already perceptible, especially in the fast-increasing globalization-process, greatly facilitated by the immigrant diasporas.[25]

[23] For example, the INALCO of Paris has quite recently been celebrating its 200 years existence as it been founded in 1777. What links does this specific institution have with the *Institut d'études politiques*, where Islam-research concerning the immigrant North African populations in France and also the other main migrant communities in other European countries has been started?

[24] See the bibliography of F. Dassetto since the publication of, *L'islam transplanté* in 1984 and the last work he coordinated, *Islamic Words. Individuals, Societies and Discourse in Contemporary European Islam*, Maisonneuve and Larose, Paris, April 2000.

[25] The diasporas have become a distinct research-field as exemplified by the Diaspora series of R. Cohen at the Cambridge University Press. In Britain, the special fact that B. Parekh

In Britain also, the Indian researchers' presence can also be observed and at times, these Indians would be considered as more numerous than the other minorities in the other European countries. But, at a closer examination of this issue, this first impression can fade away, especially in the field of immigration/Islam and citizenship. Nevertheless, this specific aspect of ethnic minority presence in these research-fields will have to be studied more closely and the comparatist approaches be encouraged between the diverse countries, inheriting from distinct political and university histories. On an institutional level, the SOAS has since the late eighties and especially since the mid-nineties been more active on the Islam-issue, but probably more so an international level, due to the rise of Islamic fundamentalism throughout the Muslim world. Universities as Oxford and also other provincial Universities and notably the specialists of the former countries from where the immigrants come have by now become the more dynamic research-milieux not only on a local national scale but also on a European/international scale (Roger Ballard, Steven Vertovec, Ceri Peach...). Edmund-Burke III,[26] one of the specialists of French Orientalism, of the Orientalism/Islam issue and also of the Maghreb, has been discussing in the early eighties, the specificities about the setting up of French administrative institutions (*Bureaux arabes*), research/social control centres (*Mission scientifique du Maroc, Ecole d'Alger*) and pinpointed also the rivalries existing between these diverse institutions.

The pre-history of French sociology and its links with orientalism

What types of intellectual links were established between Durkheimian Sociology and Orientalism? Conflicts existing in the early days of French sociology (1890-1920, *i.e* Durkheimism's origins, development and consolidation) between the Orientalists and the pioneering French sociologists, who have been working in the Maghreb seem to have been perpetuated during one whole century. Antagonistic relations exist since the official birth of French sociology. It seems that Louis

and T. Modood are currently cited by A. Favell is almost absent in French social sciences, apart from one of the pioneers of French migration-research, namely A. Sayad who has been seen here as one of Bourdieu's representatives within the French University.

[26] 'The First Crisis of Orientalism, 1890-1914', in J.-Cl. Vatin, *Connaissances du Maghreb. Sciences sociales et colonisation*, édit. du CNRS, 1984, Paris, - Phillips (C.H.), *The School of Oriental and African Studies, University of London, 1917-1967 : An Introduction*, London, Design for Print, 1967. Edmund-Burke III compares the British SOAS and the Ecole nationale des langues orientales vivantes, 'The creation of the School of Oriental and African Studies of the University of London can be seen, in a sense, as an effort to endow Great Britain with a source of expertise broadly parallel to France. But even more so than in France, the effort in Great Britain took the form of creating an entire new institution, rather than seeking to piecemeal, up-date and reform existing ones'. See also the recent historical work of Pierre Singaravélou, *L'Ecole française d'Extrême-Orient ou l'institution des marges (1898-1956). Essai d'histoire sociale et politique de la science coloniale,* L'Harmattan, Collection Recherches Asiatiques, 1999.

Massignon[27] was quite disdainful vis-à-vis the *L'Année Sociologique*'s team around Emile Durkheim. Durkheimians working in the Maghreb (namely, René Maunier, Robert Montagne) were far from negligible, but they apparently did not know how to deal with the Islamic factor and the Arab language. F. Colonna describes traditions characterising Orientalists and social scientists. After reviewing a number of specialists of the Maghreb, she concludes on a yet unresolved issue, 'Hence the question: why did none of these writers succeed in producing something 'lasting' about Islam as a religion? Answer: because they were unable to reconcile the social sciences and textual exegesis. To simplify matters: some of them were Durkheimians, but could not read Arabic. Others could read Arabic, but were so absorbed in their own studies that communicating their findings to a wider audience seemed to them to be of secondary importance. This is particularly true of Massignon, who, according to Maxime Rodinson (*personal communication*), greeted the very mention of the Durkheimians with sarcasm.' Edmund Burke III also described with more details the networks of French Orientalists, sociologists, and administrators working in North Africa and the types of relations existing between them and also with the native intellectuals. But, more vitally today, Pierre Bourdieu (who has been doing his pioneering fieldwork in Kabylia after or simultaneouly with his fieldwork on *peasant celibacy* in his native Bearn), appears to have been part of a tradition which tries, according to F. Colonna to avoid an '*embarrassing religion*.' In fact, we are unable today to assert anything worthwhile about ties or absence of ties existing between *Bourdieusian sociology* or even *Tourainian sociology* and Islam, as no specialised research-work has yet been done on these complex interrelated topics.

Concerning the Orientalist institutes working on Islam in France/Europe, only some remarks of Fanny Colonna about the traditional conflicts of interest opposing the Orientalists (philologists, linguists ...) to the social scientists have been made. Reverse movements were also observed. Such as the one introduced by Marcel Mauss, who in 1901 was appointed to a chair in the 'religions of the non-civilized peoples' at the *Ecole pratique des hautes études* and held it for the next forty years, that is, the start of World War II, almost a decade before his death in 1950. He used this observatory[28] to build *links* with anthropology and the social sciences. In the French social sciences, Mauss distinguishes himself from the other

[27] F. Colonna tries in her article, '*Islam in the French sociology of religion*,' *op. cit.*, to describe their specificities. E. Burke III, in his contribution, 'The first crisis of Orientalism, 1890-1914', in J.-Cl. Vatin, *Connaissances du Maghreb. Sciences sociales et colonisation*, *op. cit.* See also the work of L. Lowe, *Critical Terrains. French and British Orientalisms*, Cornell University Press, Ithaca, 1991 and the work of a French anthropologist of India, *L'Inde fabuleuse. Le charme discret de l'exotisme français (XVIIe-XXe siècles)*, Kimé, 1999 in order to acquire a comparatist approach of European orientalisms.

[28] As F. Colonna showed it in her contribution, in the collective work, *Le Religieux des sociologues*, L'Harmattan, 1997 and also in her, 'Islam in the French sociology...,' *op. cit.*, where she once more specifies the difficulties of the main figures of French sociology to avoid this issue. The special issue of *Awal*, Cahiers d'études berbères, n°21, 2000, *Autour de Pierre Bourdieu et de l'anthropologie*, can help to bring some more light on these interrelated questions.

Durkheimians in attempting to set up links between Orientalism (especially the field of primitive religions and Indianism) and anthropology. Mauss, informed through his close ties with one of the most illustrious French Indianists Sylvain Lévy, had a very high standard of knowledge of the Indian cultures. He showed his expertise within the Indianist domain through his almost critical comments of Célestin Bouglé's work on the Indian caste-system. Philippe Besnard, who has been doing some important work on Mauss and the rest of the Durkheimian team, also remarked upon the ease with which Mauss was discussing caste and Indian cultures with C. Bouglé, rather than dealing with the nearer Islam just across the Mediterranean Basin. On the other hand, Mauss seemed not to be, according to Lucette Valensi, at ease with the culturally and geographically nearer Moroccan Islam, illustrating the paradox of French disinterest in the nearer exotic cultures for the geographically further ones. Unfortunately, during the second World War, French sociologists paid a heavy toll. Halbwachs died in Buchenwald in 1945 and Mauss himself went distraught and died in 1950. Post World War II's French sociology,[29] went into ruins, and especially the rich traditions introduced by the late Mauss, concerning the religious factor in human society were, to a great extent, given up.

Orientalism as a specific research-field helps in understanding how during the pre-history of French/European migration-research, Islam was avoided or forgotten as an important dimension of immigrant workers' lives, despite the publication of some synthetic articles in the *Revue d'études islamiques* of the Langues O, in the twenties and thirties concerning the settlement of Maghrebian Muslim workers in the metropolis. As a specialised community on the former colonies, where the Orientalist discourse was set up essentially in France/Britain, would the Orientalists have avoided the immigrant groups during the intensification of the migration-debates within their own home-countries? Are these processes consequent to the Eurocentric colonial histories of the major sending countries? In fact, the same patterns of thought which were dominant during the early days of migration-research can be observed in the politicization of the Islam-issue in the home countries of the *Orientalists*. Such that the more traditional Orientalist teaching and research-institutions have been relatively slow to start and develop research-programs on Islam-issues at home. Another factor which may have influenced the absence of Orientalist research, is the low social status attached to the Islam introduced by immigrant workers, as it has been the case for most of French social sciences[30] in their approach of working-class immigrants.

[29] According to T. Nichols Clark, *Prophets and Patrons. The French University and the emergence of the Social Sciences*, Harvard University Press, 1973. See F. Colonna, in *Le Religieux des sociologues*, and Ph. Besnard, in a special issue of the *Revue de sociologie française*, 1979-1980, concerning the Durkheimains and also his major work, *The Sociological Domain. The Durkheimians and the Founding of French Sociology*, Cambridge University Press, Cambridge, 1983.

[30] See G. Noiriel, in his introduction of, *Le Creuset français*, Le Seuil, Paris, 1988, where he detailed these disciplinary approaches. Some of the INALCO's lecturers would become

How to link migration and Islam issues in Europe to its orientalist traditions?

How can we link up the Orientalist debates to the migration and Islam issues in Western Europe? In fact, what connections can be observed between a range of disciplines called Orientalism, set up seemingly according to the Saidian version[31] during colonization and the more recent immigrant workers' settlements in the European conurbations? The history of Orientalist studies in the different European countries can, to some extent, help in their identification. For example, how can we account for the early attraction of the Orient (namely, India)[32] on the German Romantics? And what influence had Islam in the origins and development of Orientalism, and in the Western European social sciences, such as it has been studied by the Canadian sociologist, Michel Despland for the French religious sciences? However, it must be observed that the lively debates, which have followed the publication of several books, commenting Edward Said's *Orientalism*, in the English-speaking countries, have almost forgotten France, as one of the privileged terrains of the birth of Orientalism.

In fact, apart from the translation by Catherine Malamoud and the foreword to that work of Said by Tzvetan Todorov, in the early nineties, French social sciences have remained almost outside the debates concerning that specific research-domain. The paradox is stronger, in that Said referred much more to French scholars and Orientalists, in accordance with French more deeply entrenched geopolitical influence in the Mediterranean Basin. Despite the important pioneering work that has been started by Jean-Robert Henry[33] at the IREMAM at Aix, the connections that can be established between the debates on Islam and the Orientalism-issues are still very marginal in the French University. This research-centre was initially destined to accumulate knowledge on the Arab and Muslim world, in an Orientalist sense, rather than a centre for research on Maghrebian communities transplanted Islam in France. However, the networks of Political Studies Institutes (IEP) starting a vast research on Muslim populations in France did inevitably include researchers (as Françoise Lorcerie, Jean-Robert Henry ...), former doctoral students (as Jocelyne Césari, Frégosi under the

interpretors and translators of the immigrants' documents. They may also do some pioneering research-work on the new migrant communities. But, then the fast rising specialised migration-research centres will replace these first researchers. This pattern has been observed for specialists working on the Indian communities living and working in France.

[31] K. Schipper et C. Gyss-Vermande (dir.), *Livre Blanc de l'Orientalisme français*, Société Asiatique, Paris, 1993, actes du Colloque du 10 janvier 1992, 'Pour une nouvelle politique de l'orientalisme,' see also the contribution of Ch. Malamoud, 'Critique et critique de la critique de l'orientalisme.'

[32] M. Hulin and Ch. Maillard (dir.), *L'Inde inspiratrice. Réception de l'Inde en France en France et en Allemagne (XIXe et XXe siècles)*, Presses Universitaires de Strasbourg, coll. Faustus, Etudes germaniques, 1996.

[33] J.-R. Henry and L. Martini (dir.), *Littératures et temps colonial. Métamorphoses du regard sur la Méditerranée et l'Afrique*, EDISUD, Mémoires Méditerranéennes, 1997, Actes du Colloque d'Aix-en-Provence, 7-8 avril 1997, Centre des Archives d'Outre-Mer.

supervision of Bruno Etienne and Vincent Geisser under Michel Camau) who were in the late 1980s and early 1990s starting research on Muslim populations and their political behaviours within the French political system, and who will be among the most prolific French researchers on the Islam-issues. It would be pertinent today to assess this initial network of Aix-en-Provence in its impact on migration and Islam research in France/Europe.

It seems that Germany or rather the German Empire, due to its ties with the Ottoman Empire was the first Western European country where a *mosque was built*. How was it that Germany not having important Muslim colonies was able to build the first Mosque in the second half of the 19th Century (long before Britain and France)? How was Germany also the first to set up such a powerful tradition as Orientalism and has also been the first to mobilise massively its Orientalist community in the study of immigrant Islam? The interwar years factor[34] should be reintroduced in these debates concerning Orientalism and the attractions exerted by Eastern mysticism in France and ultimately the Islam-issue. René Guénon (an Oriental mystic, who died as a converted Muslim in Cairo in the early fifties and referred to very briefly in Gilles Kepel's, *Les banlieues de l'islam*), and his intellectual influence on the young Louis Dumont (cf. the seemingly influential network of *Le Grand Jeu* in the Parisian debates), have to be rediscussed within the context of these uncertain political years of the thirties to understand the absence or weakness of the Orientalist research-traditions in Paris, compared to Germany, which was in France seen as a model especially after the 1870 War. Jackie Assayag and Roland Lardinois during their researches on the specific connections linking Louis Dumont (who founded the CEIAS[35] in 1956) with Indianism and the caste system, went into great details about the friendship between Dumont and Guénon and between Dumontian anthropology, characterised by the hierarchiral system of Indian castes, built in a comparatist approach with the German socio-political system, and Guénon's Orientalist and at times, crypto-fascist inclinations.

The French and German contexts were specific in Europe in that they did interrelate quite densely compared to the Franco-British exchanges, which are still today less dense than those between Germany and France, concerning the distinct domains of immigration and Islam. What were the reactions of the Durkheimian team in the specific social and political contexts of the pre-World War I period? It

[34] J. Touchard, 'L'esprit des années 1930. Une tentative de renouvellement de la pensée politique française,' in *Tendances politiques dans la vie française depuis 1789*, Colloques Cahiers de civilisation, (dir.) de G. Michaud, Hachette, 1960. J.-L. Loubet del Bayle, *Les Non-conformistes des années 30. Une tentative de renouvellement de la pensée politique française*, Le Seuil, 1969 ; J. Assayag, 'La construction de l'objet en anthropologie. L'indianisme et le comparatisme de L. Dumont', *L'Homme*, n°146, 1998. Concerning the close interactions between the French University and the German one, see Cl. Digeon, *La Crise allemande de la pensée française, 1870-1914*, PUF, 1st edition 1959 and L. Dumont on the German ideology, *L'Idéologie allemande. France-Allemagne et retour*, Gallimard, 1991, after his work on the Indian caste system, *Homo Hierarchicus. Essai sur le système des castes*, Paris Gallimard, 1966.

[35] Indian and South Asia Centre of Studies (Centre d'études de l'Inde et de l'Asie du Sud).

should not be forgotten that the early Durkheimism was set up in the context of the secularization of the French school (which was a Republicanist fight against Catholicism), of the political consequences of the Dreyfus' Affair and of a series of scandals as the Panama affair and the Boulangist episode. Foreign specialists[36] in the domains of the sociology and history of social sciences implicitly pointed out to the Jewishness of Durkheim, its minority status in a dominantly Catholic France and its probable consequences on his academic and political trajectory. Durkheim's republicanist political commitments would seem to have been the utmost results of his Jewish identity.

In fact, the influence of Durkheim and Mauss' Jewishness (as a minority religion in France) has not yet been properly debated in the French University milieux, as the republicanist ideologies must have most probably influenced their neutral positions in the official public spheres. It can be quite surprising that the more intimate feelings of individuals vis-à-vis their socio-religious origins and sometimes the indirect consequences on these same individuals' trajectories as intellectuals-academicians have not yet been studied. More pertinently, a preliminary assessment of Muslim intellectuals' consequences on the European Universities' discourses on Islam and the general disciplines of the social sciences and more specifically, the religious sciences should be attempted in the coming years. These unofficial, indirect or informal dimensions have not really been debated in the diverse social scientific schools of thought and seem to be prohibited by the official and at times, the more 'doctrinaire' teams. Recently, at a seminar at the EHESS,[37] concerning Mauss and his Jewish networks (as can be testified by the influence of the Indianist Sylvain Lévy's influence on young Mauss, Lévy being also the one Indianist who refused the presentation of the doctoral dissertation of René Guénon on Oriental mysticism, because of the latter's fascist intellectual inclinations), some of the Bourdieusian representatives have been harbouring some mixed feelings vis-à-vis such an ethnic (in the French context called communautarist) approach of Mauss, by the Canadian specialist on Mauss, Marcel Fournier.

British and American academic contexts are quite close (initially, through the language-medium) and intellectual interactions are quite dense. Contributions in the development of Orientalist knowledge are also brought about by most of the Northern European and Scandinavian countries, whose research-communities work in English. The Southern European countries are also now growing closer to the British and American Universities, as a growing section of their elites is now increasingly preparing their doctoral dissertation in either a British or American University. It should not also be forgotten that the Christian Churches'

[36] R. W. Connell (of Sydney University), 'Why is Classical Theory Classical', *American Journal of Sociology*, vol. 102, n°6, May 1997, University of Chicago, Chicago.

[37] Colloquy *Marcel Mauss et son réseau*, organized within the following agenda, 1) Les Durkheimiens et les Juifs en France, 2) Professeurs, collègues et amis, 3) Elèves et collaborateurs (22-24 March 2001, at University Paris VII/Maison des Sciences de l'Homme).

Organizations have played a great role in the development of sociology[38] and more specifically in the field of the sociology and history of religions. The pioneers of the Chicago university's sociology have been partly recruited among the Churches' representatives. Similarly in France, Christian missionnaries, as the Dominican Serge Bonnet have helped in developing the sociology of religion, after his work on religion and politics in the Lorraine region, and especially among the Italian immigrants in its mining areas. Another important dimension which has been perhaps only marginally studied in France is the contribution of the Christian, especially Jesuit milieux in the accumulation of knowledge on Asian Orientalism[39] and also that of the Pères Blancs in North Africa.

Orientalism has mobilised a quite vast array of researchers and research-centres throughout the Anglo-Saxon world, especially after the work of the Palestinian intellectual, Said at Columbia University. Some schools of thought have been identified and especially the ones which have links with the development of the Orientalist discourse and its connections with Islam. John M. Mackenzie[40] of the University of Lancaster, specialised in the area of Imperial History, has allowed us to have an insight of the debates concerning Orientalism. In 1996 (almost 20 years after Said's *Orientalism*), he most helpfully provides a tentative synthesis of the whole reaction to Said's book first published in 1978. Another work of importance was published in 1993, as an outcome of the 44th annual South Asia Seminar at the University of Pennsylvania in the academic year 1988/1989 on the topic, 'Orientalism and Beyond.' The organizers of the seminar, Carol A. Breckenridge and Peter Van der Veer, acknowledge that their book was largely inspired by Said's *Orientalism*, that is, 10 years after its first edition. Canada will be present in the French university-debates through their sociologists of French descent, as Marcel Fournier and Michel Despland. These sociologists are very close and intimate with the French political and academic worlds and have provided some of the best work on such topics as the sociology and history of the social sciences in their links with the religious factor, Orientalism, and Islam. However, they may be looked down by some sectors of the French mandarinate, as they are destined to bring some innovations to the traditional Parisian dominated French social sciences.

Lack of exchanges between the different European countries developing their specific social scientific discourses, their distinctive Orientalist discourses,

[38] J.-P. Williaime in his handbook, *Sociologie des religions*, PUF, 'Que sais-je?' coll., 1990, Paris, has brought to light the important contribution of the Ch. Churches' representatives in the development of sociological knowledge in the USA and in France. A discussion on the importance of the Belgian Catholic University of Louvain in the development of the European scientific debates on Islam is quite urgent in the coming years.

[39] I. G. Zupanov, 'Le repli du religieux. Les missionnaires jésuites du XVIIe siècle entre la théologie chrétienne et une éthique païenne', *Annales Histoire Sciences Sociales*, n°6, November-December 1996, pp. 1201-1223.

[40] J. M. Mackenzie, *Orientalism. History, theory and the arts*, 1996, Manchester University Press ; E. Said, *Orientalism*, 1978, Penguin Press, London ; C. A. Breckenridge and P. Van Der Veer, *Orientalism and the Postcolonial Predicament. Perspectives on South Asia*, University of Pennsylvania Press, 1993.

their citizenship and migration-research in accordance with their political histories have been some of their major features. Their migration-researches have led to deeper and fundamental questionings of the national identities, the history of their political and also educational systems. Their Orientalist schools and also their social sciences of religion complain of not receiving enough funds and more fundamentally their specialists (linguists, philologists, archaeologists ...) may despise the other rising specialists in the domains of Islam (politists and sociologists in Paris and Aix). It's a continuing conflictual debate since the origins of institutional sociology in the different European countries, especially in France. Whereas in Germany and perhaps Britain, their social sciences were nearer to their literary domains,[41] traditionally nearer to their Orientalist literary writings and colonial administrative systems. And, today within these new challenges to the different European states, new discourses on the specific integration and citizenship issues are being currently debated by university-specialists, national and grassroots' politicians and also by the stratified immigrant ethnic and more often religious immigrant leaderships across the European Continent.

Towards a redefinition of citizenship

Citizenship is constantly being defined in new ways. Its basic meaning changes according to the flow of immigrants and how communities consolidate themselves and build institutions. Globalization has the power, still underestimated, to transform national and local societies and more and more social scientists are studying its impact on citizenship. A chronology of recent key events[42] in Europe illustrates the fast-changing situation. These symbolical events have had a big effect on what sociologists call 'the European public sphere.' The many discourses of academics, government officials and community leaders cannot be understood without first grasping the sense of these interactions.

Jocelyne Césari, in her book *Musulmans et Républicains* (1998), approaches citizenship in terms of third generation French Muslims in France. Such citizenship is confined within France's national borders. But globalization seems to encourage the reconstitution of belief systems that transcend political frontiers. Events of local or regional importance have sometimes not reached beyond these national borders. The Ray Honeyford affair in Britain, discussed in

[41] W. Lepenies, *Between Literature and Science, op. cit.*; R.E. Kent for Britain, *A History of British empirical sociology*, Aldershot, Gower Publishing Company, 1981 ; and the more recent work of M. Albrow, 'The changing British Role in European Sociology,' in B. Nedelmann, (ed.), *Sociology in Europe, op. cit.* See R. Lardinois, for a quick survey of British Orientalism, namely the role of W. Jones in Fort William College in Calcutta, in, 'L'Etat colonial, les sciences sociales et le mouvement national en Inde,' in special issue of the journal, *Peuples Méditerranéens, Sciences sociales, sociétés arabes*, n°54-55, (ed.), F. Colonna.

[42] S. Rushdie in Bradford, the schoolgirls' headscarves affair in the Paris suburb of Creil, the controversy over headmaster Ray Honeyford's views in Britain and far-right racist attacks in Germany.

Steven Vertovec's article about Islam in 'the British public sphere,' is known abroad only to groups of specialists. The impact of Ambrosian Islam in northern Italy or of Catalonia Islam,[43] and the regional aspect of that within a nation-state, may well alter the debate at European level. Such regional dimensions could also, according to some pioneering students of Islam in Europe, such as Rémy Leveau, help take the issue beyond national borders.

This survey of contemporary debate about citizenship is divided into research done in France and work done elsewhere, which is dominated by English-speaking scholars. This does not mean research beyond French and Anglo-American academic circles is ignored. There are many such experts, mostly writing in English, which makes it easier to circulate their work than research done in French or other European languages. Debate about globalization and citizenship has been largely dominated by Anglo-Saxons and by French scholars of international relations, notably Bertrand Badie, who have built up a major body of work since the late 1980s.

Only major trends are noted, involving individual scholars or teams who have done long-term work on the relationship between immigration, Islam and citizenship. Over the last 20 years, research into immigration and citizenship has increased amid great politicization of immigration issues (France's Nationality Commission in 1986) and of Islam (the Rushdie affair and the suburban Paris school headscarf episode). The links between the issues of immigration among European countries, whether immigrants can vote and local democracy in poor immigrant city suburbs are becoming a political hot potato that could endanger the growth of democracy in individual countries and in Europe as a whole. In France, political scientists are probably more energetic than other scholars, especially sociologists, in researching these subjects.

French-speaking sociologists working outside France sometimes seem more dynamic – younger scholars like Marco Martiniello and his team at Liège University and Marco Guigni and Florence Passy at Geneva University. Comparative studies by robust European-level teams are on the rise.[44] The many conferences where these experts meet and build up major networks are the way things are going and greater communication through jointly-published work makes these networks, or at least their leaders, better known. Comparative research at European and Western level is now common. Individual scholars risk obscurity in their own country if they do not enter the competitive new academic environment that will make them better known internationally.

[43] S. Vertovec, 'Islam and the Public Sphere in Britain,' in G. Nonneman et al., *Muslim Communities in the New Europe, op. cit.* On the regional growth of Islam, see also R. Leveau (ed.), *Islam(s) en Europe, op. cit.*

[44] A. Favell of the Sussex Centre for Migration Research at the School of European Studies (Brighton), M. Bommes of the IMIS (Institut für Migrationsforchung und interkulturelle Studien (Osnabrück), R. Bauböck and his European Research Centre (Vienna), the Geneva University team, M. Baganha in Coimbra (Portugal), Giovanna Zincone (Turin), and R. Zapata-Barrero of Pompeu Fabra University (Barcelona). These European-level teams have been doing comparative studies for quite some time and some have even extended their activity to Australia and North America.

This survey is limited to the relationship between immigration, Islam and citizenship. We look first at the work done in France to see the situation in the country that was probably the first to develop the idea of citizenship.[45] Then there are the many younger researchers, especially Americans,[46] who came to Paris in the 1980s and 1990s to do their doctorates and mingled with the pioneers of the CERI. Their theses and articles (Myriam Feldblum, David Beriss), now published and available to an international audience, often get most attention in debate outside France. The growing internationalization of research networks means the research of world-class experts[47] inevitably looms over such debates. The younger generation have a more flexible attitude and do not behave yet like grand leaders of schools of thought. Their work contributes to truly comparative research into European citizenship issues.

The French approach

In France, the first people to write about citizenship and how it relates to immigration and Islam were mostly political scientists. The work of citizenship theorists among them, such as Jean Leca, Marc Sadoun, Dominique Colas and Nicolas Roussellier,[48] are noted. But most of the debate focuses on the more

[45] See the work of British historians on the French Revolution and the notion of citizenship, especially S. Schama, *Citizens. Chronicles of the French Revolution*, Penguin Books, London, 1989 ; E. J. Hobsbawm, *Echoes of the Marseillaise. Two Centuries Look Back on the French Revolution*, Verso, London, 1990 ; E. J. Hobsbawm and Terence Ranger, *The Invention of Tradition*, Canto, Cambridge University Press, 1983, and another book by Hobsbawm, *Nations and Nationalism since 1780. Programme, Myth, Reality*. Canto, Cambridge University Press, 1990.

[46] Probably as a result of the work of S. Hoffmann, especially the co-authored book *In Search of France*, Harvard University Press, 1960, the founding of the journal *French Politics and Society* and the research on immigration by A. Zolberg, M. Miller, M. Schain, R. Brubaker and other scholars interested in France. The importance of French Studies departments at US universities, teaching French literature, human sciences and now sub-disciplines such as post-modernist studies and gender studies as part of research into French society, needs to be reassessed.

[47] Especially the work of S. Castles, Y. Nuhoglu Soysal, M. Miller, C. Wihtol de Wenden, J. Hollifield, R. Bauböck, M. Martiniello, A. Favell, V. Amiraux, M. Bommes, A. Geddes and S. Sassen. The work of one of the younger scholars, A. Favell, who published in 1998 a comparative study, *Philosophies of Integration. Immigration and the Idea of Citizenship in France and Britain,* in the series 'Migration, Minorities and Citizenship' (University's Centre for Research in Ethnic Relations), edited by Z. Layton-Henry and D. Joly, is starting to become known.

[48] See M. Sadoun, *La Démocratie française*, 2 vol., Fayard, Paris, 2000; see also the chapter by N. Roussellier, 'Deux formes de représentation politique: le citoyen et l'individu' *in* vol. 1 and by D. Colas, 'La citoyenneté au risque de la nationalité,' *in* vol. 2. Especially important are the many articles by J. Leca written during the 1980s and 1990s, when immigration and Islam became issues in French political life, notably 'Questions sur la citoyenneté,' *in Projet*, n°171-172, January-February 1983; ' Nationalité et citoyenneté dans

'applied' work of Catherine Wihtol de Wenden (with Rémy Leveau and their doctoral students and Gilles Kepel),[49] Jean Leca, Abdelmalek Sayad, Bertrand Badie, Jacqueline Costa-Lascoux and Patrick Weil. French sociological research into citizenship centres mostly around the work of Dominique Schnapper and perhaps Pierre Rosanvallon. But French academics in various disciplines have exchanged ideas, often at the suggestion of the research team leaders. Contacts between the immigration/Islam team at CERI and the one at CADIS working on Tourainian social movements have produced results, especially where emerging social issues are concerned. These scholars looked at the political involvement of young people from immigrant families, the growing visibility of Islam, suburban violence and the strong links between the internal order of each state and the external order. The exchanges between the sociologist Schnapper and the political scientist Leveau during CERI's fieldwork in 1987-89 took place very early on and a pioneering attempt was made to compare Jews and Muslims in the French political system.[50] But work did not continue on these comparative issues now at the heart of post-Gaullist and post-Mitterrand France's domestic and foreign policy (especially towards the Arab world and ties with Israel). The recent connection in autumn 2000 between the Palestinian *intifada* against Israel and the disturbances in French cities and suburbs involving Beurs and attacks on synagogues and other Jewish symbols were significant. Reports in the daily *Le Monde* on the situation in suburbs like Trappes and especially Sarcelles, where large communities of Sephardic Jews and North Africans live side by side, reflected these interactions.

French research today is up against rapidly-changing ideas at international level that could eventually produce a kind of French isolationism. A problem has been spotted in parts of the national academic community where the concept of citizenship has been defined and some French scholars are looking at the progress foreign researchers have made here. A good proportion of French intellectuals and media still seem attached to republicanism, an ideology that draws equally from left and right to produce a peculiarly French nationalism discussed by Israeli historian Zeev Sternhell. This sometimes directly hinders intellectual contacts with other academic communities that involve the exchange of ideas that lubricate and enrich national academic and political discourse. An example of such interaction is the impact and growth in France of the concept of ethnic politics, shown by Feldblum 12 years after her fieldwork in Paris and nearly 20 years after the groundbreaking work in 1983 of sociologist Pierre-Jean Simon[51] on the profound

l'Europe des immigrations,' written for the G. Agnelli Foundation, March 1990 ; and 'La citoyenneté entre nation et société civile,' in D. Colas, C. Emeri and S. Zylberbeg, *Citoyenneté et nationalité*, PUF, Paris, 1991.

[49] *Cf. Les Banlieues de l'Islam : naissance d'une religion en France*, Seuil, Paris, 1991.

[50] 'Religion et politique: juifs et musulmans maghrébins en France,' in 'Les Musulmans dans la société française,' special issue of the *Revue française de science politique*, vol. 37, n°6, December 1987.

[51] See the work of Sternhell, supervised by political scientists in Paris such as J. Touchard and R. Girardet to understand how the study of French nationalism developed. For work on immigration and its effect on French political and academic life, see Feldblum,

influence of republicanist ideas on the use in France of notions of ethnic minorities and ethnicity. This phenomenon tends to isolate all French scholars in the field, except those at institutions such as the EHESS, the IEP and their many research teams, along with non-university bodies working in the international field, such as IFRI and IRIS (Institute of International and Strategic Relations). The participation of these institutions in international debate shuts out the classic universities. So provincial and Paris suburban universities are still very much inspired in their work and bibliographies by republicanist concepts.[52] Taking part in international networks is a vital political and university issue and also essential to the reputation of research teams and individual scholars.

The evolution of Leca's ideas, at least the beginnings, shows an introverted approach and confinement in a basically French-speaking domain, the French-North-African one. Except for Badie and some immigration experts, there is still no real research being done in France on the relations between immigration and globalization. So as the new Century begins, state-centric approaches are being tested by new analyses of citizenship arising from the socio-political and economical context of globalization. Chicago University sociologist Saskia Sassen says[53] it is pointless to analyse migration only in terms of the nation and its impact on citizenship. Looking at migration as a workforce, mainly from a narrowly economic angle, is now an old-fashioned approach.

Did Leca, in a special June 1985 issue ('Immigrés/Français') of the journal *Esprit,* speak for most French scholars? It was a time when young Beurs were entering the French public and political arena and Islam was becoming increasingly visible there. His approach, assessing the 'gains' and 'losses' of immigrants in the French political arena, would seem to be economicist reasoning, despite their symbolic importance and extent. *Esprit's* interview with Leca, in its regular feature 'French Uncertainties,' appeared under the blunt headline: 'A Feeble Capacity to Integrate.'

This inadequacy of French society and its political system where integration was concerned, already identified in June 1985, soon produced fresh thinking among leaders of the North African immigrant communities, especially those who arrived in France very young or who were born and brought up in

Reconstructing Citizenship. The Politics of Nationality Reform and Immigration in Contemporary France, State University of New York Press, New York, 1999, and P.-J. Simon, 'L'étude des problèmes des minorités et des relations interethniques,' *in* 'Minorité, ethnicité et mouvements nationalitaires,' special issue of *Pluriel*, n°32-33, 1982-1983.

52 This situation has been studied by V. Vuddamalay in 'Theoretical approaches and organizations influencing French migration research,' *in Immigration and Social Sciences in Australia, France and Germany*, edited by S. Castles, which points out that the centre of French university debate has moved away from the Sorbonne, in the Paris Latin Quarter, to the nearby Boulevard Raspail and the Rue Saint-Guillaume.

53 S. Sassen, 'Mais pourquoi émigrent-ils?' in *Le Monde diplomatique*, a report on 'Le travail mondialisé,' November 2000; see also other writings by Sassen, such as *La ville globale. New-York, Londres, Tokyo*, Descartes, Paris, 1996; *Losing Control*, Columbia University Press, New York, 1996; *Globalization and its Discontents*, The New Press, New York, 1998, and *Guests and Aliens*, The New Press, New York, 1999.

France. Intellectuals, researchers and sometimes social workers and other cultural mediators are very close to the social problems in the cities and suburbs. Because they did not pass the exams to get university research or teaching jobs for reasons unconnected with their qualifications (compared with the greater number of Turkish academics in Germany and Indians in Britain), they reproduce an almost colonial-style authority over their communities. In such places, with many immigrant associations,[54] new ideas have arisen about how to become politically active at the grassroots, especially that of new citizenship. But Said Bouamama, an advocate of these new approaches to citizenship by his fellow second-generation immigrants, was eventually challenged. The more political leaders of the immigrant associations (some of whom cannot envisage entry of their communities into the French political system) criticise such theoretical and intellectual approaches. They consider it more important to be elected to posts of responsibility in French and European politics and think mainly about the symbolic and probably material rewards when a local community leader is elected to the European parliament, as some Beur men and women have been as Greens.

But the French school of research into citizenship has branched out and borrowed from other currents of thought. Bernard Badie and Pascal Perrineau, in the introduction to their co-authored *Le Citoyen. Mélanges offerts à Alain Lancelot*,[55] focus on the key question of 'citizens outside the state.' They do not deal with immigration and Islam, but do tackle central issues such as globalization and transnationalization, the crisis of the state and its many repercussions, such as 'failed sovereignty, uncertain territoriality, questionable universalization, multiple community reinvestments, complex forms of regional integration, a troubling return to the local level and a revival of particular cultures' and the influence of these on the status of the citizen. Badie[56] did theoretical work for 10 years about the effect of globalization on citizenship. In an interview in the March-April 1997

[54] Immigrant associations have been extensively studied in two reports (*Modes d'insertion des populations de culture musulmane dans le système politique français*, MIRE/CERI, Paris, 1990, and *Associations créées dans les années 1980 par de jeunes militants issus de l'immigration: bilan de leurs activités et de l'engagement de leurs promoteurs*, FAS/CERI, Paris, 1996) done by research teams supervised by Leveau and Wihtol de Wenden. A profile of Bouamama in the 1996 report was done by a young Beur journalist. Bouamama was involved in the social movements and is one of the few young intellectuals (along with M. Abdallah and the *No Pasaran* network who has just published *J'y suis, j'y reste ! Les luttes de l'immigration en France depuis les années soixante*, Reflex, Paris, 2000) to regularly publish articles and books; he has co-edited with Portuguese-born scholar A. Cordeiro and M. Roux, *La Citoyenneté dans tous ses états. De l'immigration à la nouvelle citoyenneté*, with a preface by J. Leca, CIEMI-L'Harmattan, Paris, 1992. See also Leveau and Wihtol de Wenden, *La Beurgeoisie. Les trois âges de la vie associative issue de l'immigration*, CNRS Éditions, Paris, 2001.

[55] B. Badie and P. Perrineau (eds), *Le Citoyen. Mélanges offerts à Alain Lancelot*, Presses de Sciences Po, Paris, 2000.

[56] B. Badie, *La Fin des territoires. Essai sur le désordre international et sur l'utilité sociale du respect*, Fayard, 'L'espace du politique' collection, Paris, 1995. He then published other books and many articles in various journals.

issue of *Hommes et Migrations* with its editor, Philippe Dewitte, under the headline 'What kind of citizenship will globalization bring?' he explains how citizenship 'can no longer be confined to national territory. Multiple allegiances and citizenships in several spheres develop at local levels, in the world's major regions, in networks and diasporas. But because this process threatens national structures, nation-states may be tempted to fall back on an ethnic notion of citizenship.' Other scholars, in law and philosophy, such as Étienne Balibar, Jacqueline Costa-Lascoux, Christian Bruschi and Danielle Lochak,[57] spoke up very early in the debate.

The non-French approach

The sum of knowledge built up about citizenship in the 20-25 years of research into issues arising from immigration and Islam is very impressive. But again, because of the ever-growing mass of material, we will only look at scholars and research teams who have produced steadily during most of their careers. We will summarise the main trends of research into citizenship as transformed and redefined by immigration/Islam in Western countries. The most recent work (between 1995 and 2000) gives the best overview and is often itself a summary of other research done previously or during the same period. The internationally best-known scholars are acquainted and most have set up institutional and more often informal comparative research networks. The most comparatist scholars got into an early habit of absorbing other academic and political traditions and cultures. What typologies can we make out from these first observations? They can often be found in the national contexts in which the studies have been done and written.

But we should take a look at those pioneers who have been very internationally mobile and are familiar with many national research traditions. Do their studies, focusing on global citizenship or post-national membership, mean research confined to national contexts is irrelevant? Many researchers now move across national boundaries and their personal and professional paths turn them into 'academic nomads' sometimes unconnected with any particular national research tradition. They have been able to know and experience many intellectual and political environments and been constantly confronted by fresh issues. Their lives and careers illustrate the progress of knowledge about population movement and its political impact. From the start of their careers, they have been immigrants themselves and were very probably spurred to study immigration as a result. Stephen Castles, Yasemin Nuhoglu Soysal, Saskia Sassen, Marco Martiniello and

[57] These publications include E. Balibar's 'Sujets ou citoyens,?' *Les Temps modernes*, April-May 1984, and his essays in *Les Frontières de la démocratie*, La Découverte, Paris, 1992; J. Costa-Lascoux's 'Immigration, nationalité, citoyenneté,' Laboratoire de sociologie juridique, Université de Paris II and *De l'immigré au citoyen*, La documentation Française, Paris, 1989; Ch. Bruschi, 'Droit de la nationalité et égalité des droits de 1789 à la fin du XIXe siècle'; D. Lochak, 'La citoyenneté: un concept juridique flou,' in *Citoyenneté et nationalité. Perspectives en France et au Québec*, PUF, Paris, 1991.

other young scholars at European level are themselves part of the history and movement of immigrants.

Does this mean that, in countries with strong ties to the native soil (*terroir*), the new dimensions of migration and their effect on the study of citizenship are sometimes beyond the reach of their scholars entrenched in a national tradition and sometimes hostile to the advent and growth of new ideas in their political and intellectual world? Is Europe's biggest country, Germany, an example of this, since the work done by its scholars is rarely translated for non-German-speaking audiences? Its sociological tradition is very close to philosophy and German research has a very strong theoretical bias. The French historian Gérard Noiriel, in his book *Le Creuset français,*[58] looks at the influence of key concepts in French social sciences about immigration. He shows how 'Vidalian geography' has been a field for experiment and establishing such fundamental ideas as the Braudelian long-term. The notion of 'long-term' (*longue durée*) comes from the roots of the idea of a rural community and of settlement.

This idea (*terroir*), shared by ordinary French people and described in Eugen Weber's authoritative work *From Peasants to Frenchmen*,[59] seems to have left a deep mark on the behaviour of the French, on their political élites and on a fairly dominant group of French scholars. This probably explains the late appearance of experts on globalization and its impact on the notion of citizenship, which originally meant belonging to a national society. Some foreign experts[60] on immigration, such as Castles and his team, discuss the various research traditions in French universities, noting in 1999 the purist republican approach in the works of Schnapper. Patrick Weil is seen as representing the left's national republicanist tradition. Loïc Wacquant (of the Bourdieu school), despite his comparative work in the United States, also seems to favour the republicanist model as a path to integration. However Castles and his team (Ellie Vasta and Gianni Zappala) say republicanist orthodoxy is increasingly challenged by historians such as Noiriel, who has criticised the ideological nature of the exclusion of immigrants from French historiography. Political scientists who have studied the kinds of activism and demands emerging among second generation immigrants have questioned the orthodox model's effectiveness. The Tourainian group of researchers into social movements, led by Michel Wieviorka, also realises the contradiction between

[58] G. Noiriel, *Le Creuset français*, Le Seuil, Paris, 1988.

[59] E. Weber, *From Peasants to Frenchmen. the Modernization of Rural France, 1870-1914*, Stanford University Press, 1976, translated into French with the significant title of *La Fin des terroirs. La modernisation de la France*, Fayard, 1992.

[60] In the comparative study of France, Germany and Australia, *Immigration and Social Sciences in Australia, France and Germany*, Castles, E. Vasta and G. Zappala show a very shrewd appreciation of the various current schools of thought in French academic and political circles dealing with immigration. Foreign scholars have been surprised by the often strong links some French academics have with political and social issues. This tradition of intellectuals getting involved in political struggles, especially since the Dreyfus Affair in 1898, can be clearly seen in immigration studies and merits re-examination. Favell's articles also display an acute understanding of academic circles in France and other European countries.

ideals of equality and the everyday experience of racism and social exclusion. Scholars of immigrant origin, who personally took part in the movements of the early 1980s, have published books and articles through radical publishers and journals.

Much has been written about national belonging and citizenship. Patrick Weil and Randall Hansen's book, *Nationalité et citoyenneté en Europe* (1999),[61] shows how 'in Europe, immigration policies have also become nationality policies.' Weil says in his introduction ('Citizenship, immigration and nationality: towards European convergence') that 'the right to nationality is still, despite talk about post- and trans-nationalism, the basis of a person's identity. It marks the line between us and other people. Yet the right to nationality has been quietly underestimated in recent scholarly work. One strong school of sociological thought says citizenship becomes superfluous when economic and social rights are given to people who are legal residents but not citizens. The most developed version of this idea holds that transnational migration is steadily undermining the traditional yardstick of belonging to a nation state – citizenship.[62] Add to this the fact that permanent residents may want to identify not with the nation-state but with other institutions, such as a neighbourhood, town, province or region, and you could say the second half of the 20th century has brought us to, as Yasemin Nohoglu Soysal puts it, the limits of citizenship.[63]

But how can we categorise research on citizenship done outside France proper? Work in French-speaking Belgian, Swiss and Canadian universities tends to take a different approach to this constantly changing field. Research by English-speaking scholars fits right away into the new contexts of globalization and transnationalization, diasporas, and communities ever on the move inside areas defined by various parts of diasporas. Weil points to an influential group of sociologists that surfaced in international research in the late 1980s. Soysal, from the American tradition of transatlantic research, forcefully states in her major work *The Limits of Citizenship* (1994) that we are moving towards a 'postnational model of membership.' She has done a great deal of fieldwork in several European countries that have immigrant communities, especially on the Turks in major cities.

[61] P. Weil and R. Hansen (eds.), *Nationalité et citoyenneté en Europe*, La Découverte, Paris, 1999.

[62] Ch. Joppke (ed.), *Challenge to the Nation State. Immigration in Western Europe and the United States*, Oxford University Press, Oxford, 1998; see also Joppke's other book, *Immigration and the Nation State. The United States, Germany and Great Britain*, OUP, Oxford, 1999. W. Kymlicka also published in the late 1990s a number of studies on citizenship, notably *Multicultural Citizenship*, Oxford University Press, Oxford, 1995, and a summary article with N. Wayne, 'Return of the citizen. A survey of recent work on citizenship theory,' in *Ethics*, vol. 104, January 1994.

[63] Y. Nuhoglu Soysal, *The Limits of Citizenship. Migrants and Postnational Membership in Europe*, University of Chicago Press, Chicago/London, 1994.

Thomas Hammar, Rainer Bauböck,[64] Marco Martiniello, Christian Joppke, Stephen Castles and other scholars working internationally place the issues raised by citizenship in the modern world in fresh contexts. New concepts are continually springing up, such as personhood and human rights, postnational membership, globalization and the politics of belonging, global citizenship, denizens and margizens. Such concepts, which come from a variety of academic environments, are hard to translate. Some that appeared in the 1990s will be badly translated if simply equivalent words are systematically sought in the world's languages. These issues extend well beyond the frontiers of Europe. In 1997, with her book *La Citoyenneté européenne,*[65] Wihtol de Wenden opened up still more horizons for French and European scholars. She worked at European level *(L'Europe de toutes les migrations, L'immigration en Europe)* during the 1990s, when questions about Islam and the entry of immigrants into European politics were turning immigration into a European issue, although it was being handled at administratively mainly by sovereign nation-states.

The exchange of research and ideas at international level is inevitable in today's world, where the smallest places are affected by constant movements of people. The need for comparative approaches is felt because external schools of thought help broaden and clarify debates which, if limited to one country, would quickly become irrelevant. How can ideas and academic production compete with economic production in these symbolic exchanges between countries, especially as cause and effect of globalization? The speedy world-wide dissemination of research has become common. The doctoral thesis of Feldblum, whose fieldwork was done in Paris during the first years of CERI's research between 1988 and 1990, is a good example. The book that came out of it in 1999, *Reconstructing Citizenship. The Politics of Nationality Reform and Immigration in Contemporary France* (State University of New York Press), is cited internationally more often than the work of French scholars. The circulation of some books, internationally considered classics, even seems to be limited to particular networks of French scholars, especially those actively involved in international comparative studies. Soysal's *Limits of Citizenship* has become essential for specialists. The most recent book by Castles, co-authored with Alastair Davidson, *Citizenship and Migration. Globalization and the Politics of Belonging* (Macmillan, 2000), also responds to these new political needs that flow from globalization.

The diasporas at the heart of today's globalised economies have already become a specialist area of study (the diaspora studies course of Robin Cohen[66] at Cambridge University is an example) in the field of population movement. Badie emphasises throughout his work the disruptive implications, especially for citizenship, of groups that have long operated in several national arenas at once.

[64] R. Bauböck, A. Heller and A. R. Zolberg (eds), *The Challenge of Diversity. Integration and Pluralism in Societies of Immigration*, European Centre of Vienna, Avebury, Ashgate Publishing, Aldershot, 1996.

[65] C. Wihtol de Wenden, *La Citoyenneté européenne*, Presses de Sciences Po, Paris, 1997.

[66] R. Cohen, *Global Diasporas. An Introduction*, University College, London, 1997, and *The Cambridge Survey of World Migration*, Cambridge University Press, Cambridge, 1995.

Such traits of belonging, allegiance and citizenship in several spheres are seen with diasporas of Jews (11-15 million around the world), Chinese (22 million) and Indians (eight million), according to Peter Van der Veer,[67] an expert in religions at Amsterdam University, though these figures need updating. The French historian of Indian merchant groups, Claude Markovits, shows the presence, from the 18th Century on, of people from the Sind in key places in the world economy, such as the Panama Canal, Egypt and the Red Sea, the Canary Islands, Gibraltar and the islands and peninsulas of the old British Empire, where there are sizeable communities of East Indians. These people from the Sind are sometimes citizens of several countries at once and play an active part in the globalization of trade in specialised items such as oriental fabrics. The even more numerous Chinese diaspora should also be studied for its multiple national memberships and for how its many ethnic, linguistic and regional sub-groups handle citizenship. In Europe, the dominance of North African migrants in France (and their smaller number in other European countries) and of Turks in Germany can also be studied for how they cope with their own multiple national memberships and citizenships.

[67] P. Van der Veer, *Nation and Migration. The Politics of Space in the South Asian Diaspora*, University of Pennsylvania Press, Philadelphia, 1995; Cl. Markovits recently published *The Global World of Indian Merchants 1750-1947. Traders of Sind from Bukhara to Panama*, Cambridge University Press, Cambridge, 2000. S. Vertovec and C. Peach, who have also studied Islam in Europe, edited a book with C. Clarke. *South Asians Overseas. Migration and Ethnicity*, Cambridge University Press, Cambridge, 1990.

Chapter 2

Muslims in Italy

Stefano Allievi

Introduction

What and especially *who* are we talking about? The question arises every time the presence of Islam in Europe is discussed. In Italy, things are perhaps even more complicated than in other European countries because of local factors. Until the 1970s, Italy was a country of emigration rather than immigration, so the Muslim presence there is much more recent and therefore much less known and studied. The debate about Islam also came to Italy quicker than elsewhere – imported from other European countries rather than originating in Italy itself.[1]

The issue is also hard to tackle in Italy because of its complexity. Muslim immigrants come from very many places and a significant number are illegally in the country. In France, Muslims are overwhelmingly from North Africa (or still often considered as being from there). In Germany, Muslims mean Turks. In Britain, they are Pakistanis and Indians. But in Italy no majority group dominates or leaves its mark on visible, organised (or less organised) Islam: not even the Moroccans, who account for nearly a third of all Muslims in the country but are much less cohesive than elsewhere in Europe, less influential in the mosques than their numbers might suggest and even less influential among Muslim associations.

[1] Especially during the Gulf War (see Allievi, S., Bastenier, A., Battegay, A. and Boubeker, A., *Médias et minorités ethniques. Le cas de la Guerre du Golfe*, Louvain-la-Neuve, Academia, 1992). But over the years, some issues have been imported from France as if they were already internal Italian problems. They included the controversy over wearing the Muslim headscarf *(hijab),* which did not exist in Italy then and is still very rare today in the country's schools; the Salman Rushdie affair, even if it did not have a big effect on Islam in Italy; to some extent the fear of terrorism after events in Algeria; and the existence of support cells for Osama Bin Laden before and after the September 11 attacks in the United States. The first really 'Italian' debates on these issues came much later than elsewhere. The question of the headscarf arose in 1999, when Muslims in Turin demonstrated against the local police chief for reportedly rejecting ID photos with women wearing them, and arguments about the integration of Islam began in autumn 2000 when a serious anti-Islamic campaign began to emerge (see below).

The return of Islam?

The presence of Muslims is not totally new for Italy. Historically, they have returned.[2] Islam had already taken root in some parts of the country, especially in the south. The first 'visit' of the Saracens to Sicily, from what was called Ifriqiyya (roughly today's Tunisia), dates from the dawn of Islamic history, in 652. The conquest of the island began in 827 at Mazara del Vallo (where the country's biggest Tunisian community is today) and, completed in 902, with the fall of Taormina, even though Palermo (the 'city of 300 mosques,' as Arab traveller Ibn Hawqal is said to have called it in the time of Norman rule) and most other towns in the island had been occupied since the first half of the 19th Century. Muslims also settled in other parts of the country (the Emirate of Bari, the Muslim community in Lucera) and, more recently, small 'slave mosques' still existed in 18th Century Livorno, Genoa, Rome and Naples.

So Muslims were historically 'returning,' but sociologically speaking things were obviously quite different. The new Muslims were nothing like the proud and domineering Kalbites of Sicily and the new Islam did not arrive at the point of a sword. They came instead in the garments of poverty as meek and peaceful immigrants.

Little remains of the earlier Muslim presence. Unlike in Spain, where the memory of Al-Andalus is part of the country's history and remembered as one of its richest periods in every sense, the Islamic history of Sicily is little regarded. Recent times do not provide many other examples of 'Muslim' history. Italy did not even have any colonial involvement in Arab countries that could have generated research and knowledge about Islam. The only exception is the period of Fascism when Mussolini, at the head of his small Muslim 'empire' of Libya and Somalia, tried to play the part of a 'protector' of Islam. But what remains of this? With a mixture of seriousness and irony, we have the photos of *Il Duce* holding the 'sword of Islam' given him by the Libyan leaders; his foreign policy speeches in 1928 calling Italy not just 'a friend of the Islamic world' but also 'a great Muslim power'; the shuttling of the Grand Mufti of Jerusalem between Rome and Berlin; the encouragement given to the Oriental Institute and the magazine *Oriente Moderno*, which produced the high point of Italian orientalism; and Radio Bari's broadcasts in Arabic, the first attempt at a media policy (even before the BBC's Arabic Service). But Fascism's Muslim policy had no lasting cultural effects, good or bad. This meagre 'Islamic' history and lack of research is largely why so little has been known in Italy about Islam until now.

[2] Hence the title of my book *Il ritorno dell'islam. I musulmani in Italia* (Rome, Edizioni Lavoro, 1993), which is the first detailed study of Muslims in Italy.

Some statistics

It is hard to say how many Muslims there are in Italy. The large number of illegals (without residence permits) means the total number of immigrants can only be estimated, at probably between 1.6 and 1.8 million.

Documented Muslim immigrants (or rather, those from Muslim countries and countries with Muslim minorities, which of course tells us nothing about how Islamic or practising they are) are put at about 510,963 or 36.8 per cent of all legal immigrants in Italy. To these must be added, according to a better-known estimate,[3] another 19 per cent to include minors under 18 (without residence permits because they are mentioned on those of their parents but whose number can be calculated from other sources) and those who are waiting for permits as a result of the last regularization. This gives us a total of 608,046. To Muslims by birth must be added Italian citizens who are Muslims – those who have converted to Islam – who are fewer than 10,000, and those who have obtained citizenship through marriage or other ways (20-25,000 people at most). If we add to this an estimate, still risky, of undocumented people who could be described as somewhat established (as opposed to what might be called 'birds of passage,' people always on the move) and who are therefore interested in making religious initiatives as a group, beyond their individual needs, we arrive at a total of about 7-800,000 Muslims (people of certain or possible Muslim origin). This is a far cry from the imaginative figures and exaggerated reports sometimes seen in the media or put forward by some politicians, or even some Muslim leaders who proudly boast of one, two or more million faithful. But the figure is large enough to make Islam the second biggest religion in a country where the Catholic Church has a near-monopoly and where people are not used to religious diversity.

Most immigrants in Italy come from the following countries, shown in descending order of estimated numbers, with, in brackets, the rank among immigrant groups:

Morocco 159,599 (1st), account for nearly a third of all Muslims; Albania 142,06 (2nd), most of whom are considered vaguely Muslim, often very vaguely due to the historical ups and downs of a country that until recently was officially an atheist state); Tunisia 45,680 (7th); Senegal 38,982 (9th); Egypt 32,841 (12th); Bangladesh 20,826 (19th); Pakistan 18,259 (24th); Algeria 13,216 (28th); and Bosnia 11,869 (29th). Beyond these thirty biggest groups of foreigners in Italy are Muslims from Somalia, from other parts of former Yugoslavia, from Iran, Turkey and from Italy itself. These figures give a rough idea of the complexity of the Muslim presence in Italy and show they cannot be lumped together.

There are few Turks (in contrast to their numbers in Germany, in Central Europe from Sweden to Switzerland and in France) and few Muslims from Asia (unlike in the United Kingdom and elsewhere). Only a very small number come

[3] By *Immigrazione. Dossier statistico 2001,* published by Caritas (Rome, Anterem, 2001). This is the only Italian source that tries to determine the religious affiliation of immigrants. We have made parallel estimates in previous years and the Caritas figures differ from ours *by little* more than 10,000 so they can be considered reliable.

from Italy's former colonies (except for Somalis and a few Libyans, and unlike the situation in several European countries). Except for the Moroccans, Muslims in Italy come from a wide range of countries.

The nature of Italian Islam

Immigrants began arriving in Italy in the 1970s – after their arrival in central and northern Europe – and large numbers of Muslim immigrants did not come until later. This meant the 'Islamic presence' that developed in Italy was fairly different.

One distinction was that Muslims were publicly visible much sooner than in other countries. The first generation immigrants very quickly organised themselves, establishing prayer rooms and religious-based meeting places almost as soon as they arrived, as shown by the clear link between the first regularizations and the setting up of such religious centres.

Because they come from different countries, they cannot be easily identified with any one country or foreign situation, institutionally or by public opinion (or by Muslims themselves). This means the Muslim presence cannot be treated as a foreign policy matter, which several European countries have been tempted to do.

Very few Muslims come from Italy's former colonies, so there is no past or history either to brandish or be a burden. There is also no body of reciprocal knowledge of other Muslim cultures or even a shared pre-emigration language to fall back on.

Historical development, usually forgotten by analysts, explains some contrasts with other European experiences. Muslim immigrants arrived in Italy at a time in history and at an economic period when – unlike the labour-intensive 1960s that immigrants found in central and Northern Europe – labour was moving into the tertiary sector, craft industries and small businesses. So they are not concentrated in big factories but scattered and quite isolated in small workplaces or else work on their own, running a small shop, for example. This means a lack of places to meet, socialise or perhaps organise in a non-religious way (trade unions, ethnic associations and clubs). They were also not concentrated in towns. Sizeable urban ethnic communities are still quite rare, with a few exceptions in big cities (near railway stations, for example).

Another historical development aspect has to do with the countries of origin. Most Muslim immigrants in Italy and southern Europe arrived there at a time (the 1980s and especially the 1990s) when Islam was on (and even dictated) the agenda of these countries culturally, politically and of course religiously much more than the immigration of the 1960s and 1970s did. Back then, the emerging priorities of Muslim countries, especially the Arab states (whence came most of the Muslim immigrants to southern Europe and other countries) were (especially at the political level) nationalism, Arab socialism and Arab unity, and the most respected leaders and those who mobilised people were (or were seen as) secular figures and leaders ranging from Nasser to the Ba'ath Party – Al-Fatah, rather than Hamas, to give just one example. Today, people think and act more and more in terms of clearly marked religious categories, which are 'exported' along with the rest of the cultural baggage and are more influential than before when it comes to discussion and community organisation.

Finally, the role of religious converts seems to be more important among Muslims in Italy than elsewhere, with the cultural background they bring with them, not just in terms of the image of Islam but also in the form that immigrant associations take. They play an especially big part, at this stage, in promoting community networks, political action and Muslim cultural creativity, which would probably be different and less dynamic in their absence.[4]

All these factors have a number of consequences I have tried to sum up in this 'sociological equation':

More scattered workers and communities
\+ less ethnic and secular community activity
\+ immigration from countries with great religious fervour
= a greater cultural-religious presence.

Put simply, with few other kinds of associations or just weak ones, the mosques play a much bigger role as a network and unifying element. Even more simply, there is little choice either than between the bar and the mosque, and immigrants from Muslim countries mostly have a choice between one or the other – and they sometimes choose both (personal paths are always more complicated and contradictory than our analyses).

How is it organised?

The wide variety of countries of origin is inevitably reflected in the organisational structure of Islamic communities. There is no single mother country for all Muslims, or even for most of them, and no shared language. Not Arabic – the language most commonly used in mosques and community associations – or any other, such as Turkish or Urdu, and it is early days yet for Italian to be a unifier.

Until 1970, there was only one mosque in Italy and that was in Rome. Now there are probably between one hundred and thirty and one hundred and fifty 'Islamic places.' They include well-organised centres (only three, in Rome, Milan and Catania, are full-scale mosques, purpose built), prayer-rooms and reception centres. Other places are makeshift or temporary. One Islamic source says there are more than three hundred mosques in all, which is probably optimistic. But there are still not enough to meet public demand.

Where a community is responsible for establishing these places, it is usually the Moroccans, but there are also Tunisian, Algerian, Iranian, Egyptian, Turkish, Pakistani, Somali and even Italian mosques. But there is often no ethnic network behind these mosques. This was especially true in the early days of Islam

[4] See S. Allievi, *Les Convertis à l'islam. Les nouveaux musulmans d'Europe*, Paris, L'Harmattan, 1998.

taking root in Italy. Places of worship were often set up by community groups, notably through the Union of Muslim Students in Italy (USMI, which is a member of the International Islamic Federation of Student Organisations – IIFSO), which played a big part in opening mosques in university cities, especially in the 1970s, before the arrival of large numbers of Muslim immigrant workers. Some Islamic centres, such as one in Milan, are now considered 'historic' and play more than just a local role, and there are major regional networks – in Lombardy, Veneto, Trentino, Emilia and Campania). Ethno-national networks play a role especially where there is a linguistic and sometimes religious aspect that sets them apart from the majority Arabic-speaking communities, such as those involving Somalis, Senegalese, Turks and Pakistanis. Then there are clubs, which are less common than in other countries and usually have very little influence in the wider community.

Among what could be called the rival 'religious families' – or at least parallel ones in relation to the Sunni majority and also in organisational terms – are the Shiites (nearly all of them Iranians, some Lebanese and recently a few Pakistanis, plus a very active group of converts), the Ismaelites (a socially-integrated little group unrelated to the situation of other immigrants) and a few members of non-orthodox groups, such as the Ahmadiyya and the Baha'i.

Belonging to *turuqs* – with the notable exception of the Mourides,[5] who are important both religiously and as a network of social integration and protection and economic advancement for most Senegalese, who have their own places of worship, *dahira* – seems to be more a characteristic of converts than born Muslims.[6]

More publicly, familiar, but not necessarily very strong in terms of number of affiliated groups, are the Islamic movements which, whether political or religious, are starting to appear among Italy's Muslims. They are still quite small and not yet firmly established. The Jama'at at-Tabligh, for example, is becoming influential and sure mosques, mainly in north central Italy, are linked to the movement. A different kind of movement (passing from a purely religious one to a clearly political one) is the Muslim Brotherhood, which is more important as an ideological beacon than an organised political structure. Of course within it is a hard core of militants, with close ties to the USMI and more importantly the UCOII, for which they serve as a kind of reservoir producing and breeding (or stocking up) community leadership mainly from a certain generation (the first generation of organisers of Islam in Italy in the 1970s and former students who

[5] See O. Schmidt di Friedberg, *Islam, solidarietà e lavoro. I muridi senegalesi in Italia*, Turin, Fondazione Agnelli, 1994.

[6] In Italy are found two branches of the Tijaniyya, the first Senegalese and the second Arab and mainly converts. The Burhaniyya – an Egyptian *tariqa* whose European headquarters is in Germany, and the Italian *zawiya* in Rome – are also present among some groups of converts. Converts comprise nearly all those groups linked to the Naqshbandiyya (three branches, including one led by Sheikh Nazim), to the Darqawiyya (especially the offshoot that produced the small militant group, the Murabitun) and to the Ahmadiyya Idrissiyya. There are also some members of the Alawiyya (of Algerian or Schuonian origin) and others such as the Jerrahi, from Turkey.

stayed on in Italy after university studies). A small group of Milli Görüs is also found among the Turks. Probably more important than the structured movements, with a few exceptions, are the 'cultural trends,' such as the *salafiyya,* that are based more on 'elective affinities' than seriously organised networks, though this does not stop them making domestic and foreign ties. Islam in Italy also includes other movements such as Jama'at i-Islami and also references that immigrants from each country can use from (sometimes fundamentalist) movements and parties from their home countries or in symbolic battles on behalf of the entire Muslim world (Hamas, in the case of Palestine, or the jihad fighters in Chechnya, Afghanistan and Bosnia). But it is hard in these cases to distinguish between militant support and structured organisation – or rather it would be dangerous to mix them up.[7]

More active than these are local associations that organise social activities and sometimes 'dialogue.' There is plenty of room for all these social players, who can be called, for want of anything better, freelances, who are more presenters and explainers (of Islam) than serious intermediaries between Italians and Muslim immigrant communities. Among them are some converts, who also play a very important and active part in community networks and in the job of presenting and legitimising Islam (through political relationships, the Muslim press and organising debates, for example).

Finally, we must not forget Islam's unorganised (or less organised) 'silent majority' – sociological Islam, it might be called – which is just as important in building and even reproducing European Islam. It is not found much in the networks we have listed but exists mostly at local level, and in special-interest community groups, which are not always clearly religious and not necessarily visibly 'Islamic.'

Debate about Islam

Muslims are beginning to see themselves as permanent features of Italian life and indeed their presence is starting to be seen as normal and 'inevitable'. At both local (in towns and regions) and national level, people are now facing up to what it means to have Muslims 'among us.' Surprise and questioning – and sometimes rejection instinctive at first (or rather, less organised) and now usually politically manipulated – in neighbourhoods, workplaces, schools, hospitals, prisons and churches (especially the Catholic Church)[8] quickly changed into a quest for

[7] As is often done when fundamentalism is talked about. For discussion of this, with reference to the Italian and European situation, see: S. Allievi, D. Bidussa, P. Naso, *Il Libro e la spada. La sfida dei fondamentalismi*, Turin, Claudiana, 2000.

[8] It must be remembered that in Italy much of the work of receiving immigrants is done by Catholic bodies, such as Caritas, that were the first to 'discover' Islam in their reception centres, along with new and unexpected problems they had to explain and deal with – matters of diet, availability of places of prayer, how to organise Ramadan and the tricky problem of celebrating Eid el-Kebir.

information and training, notably from teachers, social workers, religious milieux and, of course, public institutions including police.

Rather naively, and very quickly, since Islam manifested itself visibly right from the start without waiting to take deep root or waiting for a second generation, discussion began about the place of Islam in the society, or its institutionalisation, perhaps before it was ready for it. For a long while at the beginning, the debate was calm and undramatic, but in recent times sharp resistance has emerged, sometimes reflected in the media and equally among some sectors of Catholicism as among non-Catholics.

Politically, there was the very tough and often crude 'autumn campaign' against Islam by the Northern League and its leader Umberto Bossi which began in September 2000, with a series of rallies which increased after the September 11 attacks in the United States. The campaign began with a meeting and then a demonstration against plans to build a mosque on land donated by the council in the small town of Lodi, near Milan. Very offensive slogans were used and League members were even proud of gestures such as pouring pig urine over the land in question. The League conducted a fierce campaign in its daily paper, *La Padania.* It included a demonstration in Verona called 'Stop Islam,' which used the old argument from the Middle Ages about the 'promiscuity' of the Prophet Mohammed and about Islam being heresy and the modern incarnation of the Antichrist. The demonstration was cancelled at the last minute at the insistence of the League's political ally, Silvio Berlusconi.

The campaign reached a point that in November 2000, in the small town of Rovato, near Brescia, Muslims were forbidden to go within fifteen feet of a church. The order was obviously illegal, apart from being unenforceable, but was symbolically signed by the mayor, a League member, as a protest against the ban in some countries on non-Muslims from entering mosques.

More recently, especially in medium-sized League-ruled towns such as Varese and Bergamo, there have been calls to close down existing places of prayer, anti-Muslim demonstrations (the biggest was in Milan in December 2001 featuring Bossi himself) and lobbying of institutions against the permanent presence of Muslims. The League was also still, in December 2001, strongly opposed to mention of racism or xenophobia in the European plan to create international legal instruments about the fight against terrorism, to the point that Italy risked being left out of the plan.[9]

The best-known examples of the intellectual debate about Islam, from secular or non-secular sources, which led to wide debate in the media and the country, include harsh statements about Islam by the bishop of Bologna, Cardinal Biffi, who in a pastoral letter to the city and also at a press conference in early September 2000, called on the government to encourage Catholic, or at least Asian immigrants, but not Muslims. His remarks set off huge discussion, inside and

[9] French extreme right-wing leader J.-M. Le Pen lost his seat in the European Parliament because of remarks about Jews that were rather mild compared with those made by some of the League's Euro-MPs, (such as Mario Borghezio, unofficial leader of the anti-Islamic protests), and even Bossi himself about Muslims.

outside the Catholic Church, which had the useful effect of revealing the very different views of other bishops, such as Milan's Cardinal Martini and Cardinal Cè in Venice, and a large part of organised Catholicism, such as Caritas. But some of the Catholic clergy, including senior members of the Italian Conference of Bishops, supported Biffi's position.

Another example of the debate came from a secular source, in the form of a book published at about the same time by Giovanni Sartori,[10] a well-known and very influential political scientist who, as part of a critique of multiculturalism, launched into a tirade against Islam full of crude and very ill-informed prejudices, claiming that since social integration of Muslims was impossible, they should be refused entry into the country to avoid an upsurge of 'defensive' racism which, he said, would be quite justified. Even tougher words, which had much greater public impact, came in a very long article by Oriana Fallaci in *Corriere della Sera,* the country's biggest circulation daily newspaper, called *La rabbia e l'orgoglio* (the Rage and the Pride), which appeared soon after the September 11 attacks and which was made into an instant book.[11] It was a very violent and very ill-informed attack on Islam and Muslim immigration that was extremely well received and commented on by a large section of public opinion and also by intellectuals and politicians, especially those allied to the ruling coalition government.[12]

The issue of representation

For the time being, there is a discussion (still in its early stages) of the implications, at an institutional level, of the Muslim presence. Unlike what happened in Spain, which signed an *Acuerdo* (agreement) about the rights of Muslims in 1992 (though it was very hard to implement), in Italy debate about a similar *Intesa* with the Italian state has hardly begun, is a long way off and even less likely to win approval anyway.[13]

The collective social players involved in how to depict Islam are quite numerous and strongly disagree among themselves, which is a big obstacle to any

[10] G. Sartori, *Pluralismo, multiculturalismo e estranei*, Milan, Rizzoli, 2000.

[11] O. Fallaci, *La Rabbia e l'orgoglio* Milan, Rizzoli, 2001, up to now, the most selled bok on (against) Islam in Italy.

[12] For a detailed comment on these positions, with separate chapters on the positions of Fallaci and Sartori, see S. Allievi, *La Tentazione della guerra*, Milan, Zelig, 2001.

[13] The system of state supervision of religion in Italy (very similar to Spain) consists of special agreements with the majority religion, Catholicism (the *Concordato*), and agreements to guarantee the rights of minority religions (the *Intese*) that have so far been signed with the main Protestant minorities and the Jewish community. The Jehovah's Witnesses and the Buddhists also signed an *Intesa* with the centre-left D'Alema government in 1999, but these accords were not ratified by the new centre-right parliament and the Berlusconi government, which show little interest in them. On the juridical situation of the Islam in Italy see S. Allievi and F. Castro, The Islamic presence in Italy: Social Rootedness and Legal Question, in S. Ferrari and A. Bradney (eds.), *Islam and European Legal Systems*, Aldershot, Ashgate, 2000, p. 155-180.

kind of *Intesa.* At present, no Islamic organisation or group is in a position to assume clear leadership of Islam in Italy.

The main social players involved are:

- The *Centro islamico culturale d'Italia.* This was behind the building of the Monte Antenne mosque in Rome and is linked to the *Rabita al-alam al-islami*, the Saudi-dominated. Muslim World League. The mosque, claimed to be the biggest in Europe, was inaugurated in June 1995 amid great media attention. It was also reported on in several Muslim countries, for whom the building of a mosque at the very heart of Christianity, or at least in such a well-known centre of its power, was very symbolic. The *Centro* could be described as diplomatic-statist Islam, since its governing board comprises the ambassadors of various Muslim countries. However, it is financially and administratively controlled by the Saudis (despite recent strong objections by the Moroccans and changes in its management), as are most Islamic centres in European capitals.
- The *Unione delle comunità e delle organizzazioni islamiche in Italia (UCOII).* Founded in 1990, the UCOII is a new player on the Italian Islamic scene. But behind it are older organisations, starting with the Islamic Centre of Milan which, since it was set up in 1977, has been one of the best organised centres in the country and one that is very radical, compared with the Islamic centre in Rome. Also behind it is the *Unione degli studenti musulmani in Italia* (USMI), the student union that is the oldest Muslim federation in Italy, dating from 1971. The USMI is currently in decline because of the drop in the number of foreign students in Italy but is still important as a source of leaders for Islam in Italy. The UCOII, with a large number of affiliated mosques and associations, is the most representative body among Muslims in Italy and also the one most actively in contact with the media. But it is far from having control over organised Muslims and even less over Islam in Italy. However, it is the most active group and was the first one to submit to the Italian state a proposal for an *Intesa* to legally deal with the religious problems of Muslims. It also set off public debate about the matter.

Other groups, run by converts (who play a decisive role in this matter and also in the organisations just described), have shown interest in joining the battle to win recognition for Islam as part of an *Intesa.* They bring with them very controversial baggage compared with other organisations and with what could be called the Islam of the immigrants. One group is the *Associazione Musulmani Italiani* (AMI), which represents a small group of converts in Rome and is less active these days. The second and more important group has been intensely lobbying Italian institutions and is very involved in cultural activity and promotion. This is the *Comunità Religiosa Islamica* (CO.RE.IS, which plays on the fact that this acronym sounds like the word *Quraysh,* which was the clan of the Prophet), based in Milan, linked to an esoteric current of Islam. It has recently become more visible since being recognised by some institutions and getting substantial funding from the Saudis.

The *Consiglio Islamico d'Italia* was a first attempt (initially in 1998 and then in 2000) to create a single voice among Italy's Muslims, representing the main Islamic groups, which would be a partner of the Italian state in negotiations for an *Intesa*. It comprises members named mostly by the UCOII and the Islamic Centre in Rome, which were very keen on setting it up. Most of its members are also converts, including those who represent the Italian branch of the *Rabita*. The CO.RE.IS refused to join it and fierce disputes between the two groups have been clearly visible at public meetings organised by non-Muslims, so it still seems rather weak at the base and far from its goal of being the official representative of Muslims.

The role of Muslims today

Apart from the issue of representation, which excites the leaders of the various associations but ordinary Italian Muslims much less, there still seems to be little thinking or figuring out by Muslims of their role in building an 'Italian' Islam able to take into account a special context and situation that is neither the same as in their countries of origin or in other European countries that have a greater or more obvious Islamic presence.

Associations and mosques are active locally, but there is still not enough energy and production, for example, at a cultural level,[14] with a wider influence able to produce a self-aware and truly influential leadership and relieve Islamic activism of the burden of external influences. That is, the burden of movements and organisations that have a special interest in militant Islam and which try to hide as much as possible a visibly activist attitude on the internal scene so as to better 'protect' their activities directed at the outside. An attitude that weakens the ability to promote and develop a truly local Islam.

It is probably still a bit too early, in view of the short while Islam has been present in Italy, to expect a level of organisation and cultural maturity that needs more time to emerge, as a new generation and new leaders come up. The diversity of Islam in Italy, though it creates organisational problems, could be an advantage and important chance to avoid the mistakes made by some European countries in handling their own Islamic presence, which has been either too centralised or else too externalised, referring back to the main countries of origin for guidance about how to deal with it. But the religious and social needs of the Muslim community and its need to relate to the non-Muslim population are already very clear and have to be tackled. This is just not being done.

[14] Attempts to publish Islamic magazines, for example, have so far failed, except for publications that are little more than newsletters or house magazines.

Chapter 3

Foreign Immigration Comes to Spain: The Case of the Moroccans

Bernabé López García

Introduction

Spain is grappling with immigration more than 30 years after the rest of Europe. The influx of immigrants in the 1960s and the wave of family reunification in the late 1970s passed it by because its economic problems made it an unattractive destination. Immigrants finally started arriving in the late 1980s after Spain joined the European Community as a stable, democratic and increasingly prosperous state. But these immigrants were different. They were younger, many were women, and they were more skilled or at least more educated, reflecting a new situation in their home countries, where economical structural adjustment policies had led to high unemployment among college graduates, and where a women's revolution was beginning job-wise in towns and cities.

Until recently, Spain was a country that people emigrated from, as shown by the 2.5 million Spaniards who today live abroad. It has suddenly become a country of immigrants, though, at the end of 1999, it still had only 801,329 legally-residing foreigners out of a total population of 39 million. Of the 719,647 official foreign residents a year earlier, 41 per cent were from the European Union, 20 per cent from the Americas (88 per cent of these from Latin America) and 20 per cent from North Africa (94 per cent of them from Morocco). Asians comprised 8.5 per cent (a third of them Chinese) people from the Sahel countries 4 per cent, with the rest from eastern Europe and other places. Legal foreign residents accounted for less than 2 per cent of Spain's population in 1999.

Immigration quotas and laws about undocumented people

When Spain began to receive significant numbers of immigrants from Morocco, some Sahel countries, the Philippines and Central America in the late 1980s, it had an aliens law implemented in June 1985 (six months before it joined the European Community) which limited the rights of immigrants and did not encourage their assimilation into Spanish society.

Its inadequacy became clear as immigration increased and the first family reunifications took place. Government measures tried to adapt it to the new situation, since immigration seemed vital for Spain's economy in the 1990s. The demand for foreign labour grew, especially in agriculture, domestic service, construction and the hotel industry, as unemployment fell and Spanish workers began turning their backs on certain kinds of work. The left-wing government introduced a quota system that its conservative successor continued. Such quotas, which ranged between 20,000 and 30,000 foreign workers a year, were in effect regularization measures. Initially meant to benefit new immigrant workers, they were a way of legalising those who had illegally entered the country. More than half those regularized each year through such quotas already lived in Spain.

Table 1. Regularization of Moroccans 1991-1999

	Applications	Approvals	Moroccans	Moroccans
Regularization, 1991	128,127	110,067	49,089	44.6 %
Family reunification, 1992	6,777	5,881	1,623	27.6
Quota, 1993	6,000	5,220	663	12.7
Quota, 1994	36,725	22,511	7,878	35.0
Quota, 1995	37,206	19,953	8,387	42.1
Special regularization, 1996	24,637	19,634	6,479	33.0
Quota, 1997	64,174	24,585	9,281	37.6
Quota, 1998	62,697	28,095	11,131	39.6
Quota, 1999	97,034	37,678[1]	11,330[2]	38.1[2]
Total	**463,377**	**273,624**	**105,861**	**38.68**

Source: Anuarios de Migraciónes, Subdirección general de Migraciónes, Madrid, 2000.

1. The 1999 quota was 30,000. Anyone outside that was considered under general rules.
2. Provisional figures and referring to an official total of 29,764.

Between the 1991 regularization measure and passage of the new Law 4/2000, two special regularizations took place (1992 family reunification and 1996 regularization), as well as six 'recruitment' campaigns for sectors short of labour (farming, construction, domestic and other services) and quotas for each of these sectors. In 10 years, 463,370 foreigners requested regularization but not all were undocumented people. In theory at least, quotas enabled the settlement in Spain of a substantial number of people who had entered the country and then become undocumented because of official slowness in granting residence permits. Out of half a million applicants, 273,634 (including 105,861 Moroccans, the biggest nationality among them) eventually obtained permits. The new aliens law in 2000 was accompanied by another regularization measure between March and July that year. It was the country's biggest ever and involved 243,392 applicants.

Before we look at the results of this regularization, let us see (Table 2) how the quotas in recent years were directed to what kind of jobs.

Table 2. Recruitment quotas of Foreign workers

Year	Agriculture	Construction	Domestic Service	Other	Total
1995	7,855		12,091		**19,946**
1997	7,335	494	14,296	2,522	**24,647**
1998	8,700	941	14,662	3,792	**20,085**

If we break down the last year's quota into country of origin, we can see speciality by country (Table 3).

Table 3. 1998 quota by country of origin

	Agriculture	Construction	Domestic service	Other	Total
Morocco	6,760	551	2,798	1,022	**11,313**
China	82	23	1,783	1,135	**3,023**
Ecuador	176	37	1,883	149	**2,245**
Dom. Rep.	10	7	1,750	69	**1,836**
Romania	174	83	594	157	**1,008**
Philippines	1	1	984	20	1,006
Total	**8,700**	**941**	**14,662**	**3,792**	**28,095**

We can see that most Moroccans work on farms (65 per cent), the Chinese in services (more than 90 per cent) and Ecuadorans in domestic service (80 per cent), like Dominicans (most of them women) and Filipinos. Earlier years showed the same pattern. In 1992, the country in second place was Peru, with 2,520 work permits, 94 per cent of them for domestic servants.

So Morocco is the country supplying the majority of immigrant workers, most of them in agriculture and cattle-raising (70 per cent), which means they chiefly live in the coastal Mediterranean regions, stretching from Almería to Gerona, though Madrid is where the service jobs are.

Foreign immigration: an economic necessity for Spain

The front-page headline in the Spanish daily paper *El País* on 3 October 1999 was 'Spanish government preparing to receive a million foreign workers in three years,' with the sub-heading 'Labour Ministry to sign agreements with Ecuador, Mali, Poland, Romania and Colombia'. The next day, the Ministry did its best to deny the news, but the media competed to find the most 'scandalous' figure to shock their readers. *El Periódico* in Barcelona gave a figure of 1.5 million and a few days later, a moderate and intelligent pro-government commentator, Miguel Herrero de Miñón, put it as high as three million.

But the reports stemmed from several misunderstandings. The first was about an estimate of the need for labour in farming and construction, to fill jobs largely refused by Spaniards and for which foreign workers were crucial. Employers put these needs at about 300,000. But the figure did not add from year to year and at the end of three years, it would still be 300,000, not a million.

The second misunderstanding was over two agreements the Spanish government signed on 30 September but with very different partners. One was an administrative accord between the Labour and Social Affairs Ministry and the Moroccan Social Development and Labour Ministry about seasonal workers (that contained no indication at all about the possible number). The other was a protocol appended to a framework cooperation agreement between the same Spanish Ministry, trade unions and agricultural employer organizations aimed at 'regulating internal migration' in seasonal labour recruitment and adding 'subsidiary measures' to provide flexibility in hiring once the supply of Spanish, European Union and other legal foreign labour had been exhausted. The agreement in fact provided for 'hiring workers in their country of origin for seasonal farm jobs'.

For the Spanish government, the new and positive feature in this second agreement was the involvement and shared responsibility of trade unions and agricultural employers in an area as sensitive as immigration, one little understood by the public in a country where unemployment in previous years had been between 20 and 22 per cent. It was no surprise, however, that this 'positive' element escaped the attention of the media.

For more than a decade, foreign immigrants have been doing seasonal farm work in Spain, for the most part completely illegally and without any protection against being exploited. The government's aim, which officials doubt can be achieved in the next few years, is to make employers respect the terms of the labour contracts (housing, transport, social security contributions) under the watchful eye of trade unions monitoring working conditions. Despite the stand of the agricultural employers' organizations, individual farm-owners continue to duck their obligations, so the labour market continues to be a free-for-all. Only a few employers in a few provinces such as Lérida seem to have started obeying the rules by providing seasonal workers with decent housing.

But areas where immigrants have been established longest, and which are now very popular with foreign seasonal workers, are oddly where it is hardest to impose proper working conditions. A few months after the February 2000 anti-foreigner disturbances in El Ejido (Almería), no seasonal jobs were to be had there because of the obligation on employers to include housing, transport, social security and other guarantees. The employers preferred to hire day labourers each morning in the village square, as they did a Century ago. Then as now with foreign workers, it is deemed preferable to be able to choose from a surplus of manpower.

This is a tradition as ancient as the Spanish countryside, all the more striking because the sons of the old day labourers are today behaving just like the bosses of the past.

Legal non-EU foreign workers totalled 190,643 on 31 December 1998 (1.2 per cent of the active population) and were involved in agriculture (18 per cent), industry (7 per cent), construction (8 per cent) and services (63 per cent). North Africans accounted for 40.7 per cent of them.

Table 4. World-wide origin of foreign workers in Spain in 1995 (%)

North Africa	29.3
European Union	25.1
South America	16.6
Far East	9.8
Central America	6.9
Rest of Africa	5.8
Eastern Europe	3.3
North America	1.3
Middle East	0.7
Japan	0.6
EFTA countries	0.4
Oceania	0.1

Source: Inmigración y trabajo 1995, Colección OPI.

Ten countries provided two-thirds of all foreign workers in Spain.

Table 5. Country origin of foreign workers in Spain in 1995 (%)

Morocco	27.8
Portugal	6.2
Peru	6.1
Dominican Republic	5.2
United Kingdom	5.5
Germany	4.6
Argentina	4.1
Philippines	3.8
China	3.3
France	3.3
Others	29.8

Immigration as a source of unease

Spain came late to the world of immigration and the attitudes of Spaniards are behind the times too. Though still very few (less than 2 per cent of the population), immigrants of all origins became steadily more visible in Spain throughout the 1990s. They were more noticeable because the country has no recent major colonial history and has been quite politically isolated, without much contact at all with foreigners, such as those now living in Spain, apart from the mass of foreign tourists the country has got used to in recent decades.

This visibility has been heightened by a media obsessed with conflicts over immigration. Ever since the 1991 regularization measure and the appearance of the first *pateras*[1] during the summer of 1992, the illegal entry of immigrants has been a big topic in the press and on television, which have reported various local conflicts (Fraga 1992, Terrassa 1999 and El Ejido 2000) and thus helped stir up public anxiety that eventually became a political issue.

When Spain signed the Schengen Area agreement in 1991, which required a visa from nationals of certain countries, notably Morocco and other North African states, the political parties tacitly agreed, in the form of a parliamentary resolution, not to make immigration a political issue, out of respect for the millions of Spaniards who had emigrated to other countries in the 1960s and 1970s. This accord worked fairly well at government level until late 1999, when parliament debated a proposed new immigration law. It was the government party itself, the Partido Popular, which opposed the draft law being presented to parliament and tried to prevent it being passed. It lost that battle and made a stricter law part of its campaign for the March 2000 parliamentary elections.

It highlighted how many illegal immigrants were arriving in the country each day, the number of *pateras* intercepted and incidents involving immigrants. The campaign was reported by all the media and helped prepare public opinion to support amending the law to restrict the rights of undocumented aliens. The new version of the law was approved by the government in July 2000 and by both houses of parliament in December that year.

The extent of illegal immigration

The enactment of law 4/2000 of January 2000 on the rights and liberties of foreigners in Spain and their incorporation into its society was accompanied by regularization of those who had entered Spain before 1 June 1999. The regularization, between 21 March and 31 July revived argument about how many illegal immigrants there were and how many more would be drawn by the new law.

The conflict was different to 1991, when those who exaggerated the number of illegals so as to highlight the issue faced a government that tried to play

[1] Flimsy fishing boats also used for carrying passengers. As immigrant traffic grew, they were equipped with outboard motors or replaced by motorised rubber dinghies.

things down. The media and several NGOs joined in the argument, mostly on the side of the exaggerators. The 1991 regularization showed that the number of requests for regularization did not bear out either of these extreme positions and was somewhere in between. It also helped to reveal a good many of the undocumented immigrants, so the quotas and special regularization of 1996 made official figures on resident foreigners more credible, in contrast to the doubt and suspicion they had aroused in the early 1990s.

On 31 December 1999, resident foreigners in Spain totalled 801,329, including 356,216 Europeans, 90.7 per cent of them EU nationals (322,955 – 40.3 per cent of all foreigners). Add to this last figure the 3.84 per cent of the total (30,779) from other rich European countries (Switzerland etc.), the United States, Canada, Australia and Japan, and you get a figure of 55.8 per cent (447,595) of immigration that is 'disturbing' (from developing countries) Moroccans, a group that TEIM surveys have focused on, accounted for 36.1 per cent (161,870). Table 6 shows that 'non-disturbing' immigration increased faster until 1995, when the trend began to reverse itself.

Table 6. Growth of immigration to Spain 1992-1998

Origin	1992	1995	1998	% increase	
				1992-95	1995-98
Europe etc.	196,984	255,702	330,528	29.8	29.3
Rest of world	196,126	244,071	389,119	24.4	59.4
Total	**393,100**	**499,773**	**719,647**	**27.1**	**43.9**

Source: Anuarios Estadísticos de Extranjería 1992-98.

The 2000 regularization measure enabled illegal immigrants to come out of hiding. The battle over the figures was not fought in the same way as in 1991, but the media publicised an unfounded estimate of 400,000 undocumented aliens.[2] The number of foreigners who were regularized totalled 244,713, double what officials expected, but barely half the figure published in the media. By 11 December 2000, a total of 218,889 applications had been processed, including 134,509 granted and 78,701 rejected (as well as 5,556 not acted on and 123 other cases). This meant 36 per cent of applicants remained undocumented and in limbo because they did not meet the requirements. Table 7 breaks these figures down by nationality, showing the dominance of Moroccans.

[2] *El Pais* of 19 March 1997 cited 'official sources,' which was not accurate. Two days later, the head of an NGO used the same figure in an article in the same paper.

Table 7. Applications under the 2000 regularization, by nationality

	Considered	Granted	Rejected	No action	Total
Morocco	31,468	16,888	1,038	13,146	**62,540**
Ecuador	15,585	1,394	307	3,242	**20,528**
Colombia	10,705	1,564	254	1,545	**14,068**
China	5,898	2,390	1,333	1,817	**10,238**
Romania	5,558	2,020	129	1,231	**8,938**
Algeria	4,081	1,045	501	2,530	**8,157**
Senegal	2,995	2,303	140	1,206	**6,644**
Pakistan	2,175	1,760	144	2,039	**6,118**
Nigeria	1,563	2,668	40	722	**4,993**
Poland	2,478	486	47	593	**3,604**
Ukraine	2,065	570	215	674	**3,524**
Mauritania	1,502	1,055	59	333	**2,949**
Brazil	2,156	301	52	418	**2927**
Bulgaria	1,742	322	53	718	**2,835**
Argentina	2,193	221	45	355	**2,814**
Ghana	734	1,462	18	415	**2,629**
Russia	1,423	377	217	572	**2,589**
Cuba	1,912	167	55	185	**2,319**
Peru	1,651	166	43	214	**2,074**
Rest	16,648	5,746	587	32,052	**55,039**
Total	**114,538**	**42,905**	**4,077**	**64,007**	**225,527**

Source: Dirección General de Migraciónes

These figures throw a sober light on the public impression of a 'threatening flood' of immigrants given by media commentators. With the latest regularizations, about a million foreigners live in Spain, just 2.5 per cent of the total population of 40 million.[3]

But to really offset this public feeling, more is needed than just counting the number of immigrants. The pressure of immigration must be measured too. How? By visa applications? Intercepted *pateras?* Requests for asylum? Results of the quota policy? 'Guesstimates' of how many people are waiting on the other side of the Strait of Gibraltar for any illegal chance to cross?[4]

[3] 'Spain now has 40 million inhabitants thanks to immigration,' said *El Pais* on 13 December 2000. C. Alcaide, head of the National Statistics Institute, says the expected drop in Spain's population has been cancelled out by the influx of immigrants.

[4] *El Pais* reported on 6 May 2000 that 'the government reckons there are 25,000 Moroccans waiting to enter Spain'. In fact that estimate was by the Spanish government representative in Ceuta, who said 15,000 Moroccans and 10,000 people from Sahel countries were waiting to enter. The second figure may have been based on estimates by Moroccan officials published in the Moroccan press. But the first was completely arbitrary because 'intentions' are quite impossible to measure. Two days later, the paper carried an editorial about 'the

How accurately do these figures measure immigrant pressure, starting with visa applications? Spain introduced compulsory entry visas on 15 May 1991 for North Africans and citizens of some Latin American countries to curb a sharp rise in immigration from these regions between 1985 and 1990 due to inadequate laws that combined laxity and arbitrariness. For example, data from Moroccan consulates that TEIM consulted in compiling its *Atlas de la inmigración magrebi en España*[5] showed that 24,393 Moroccans entered the country during this period, while official figures showed that the number of foreign residents grew by only 10,800. The consular figures also showed that some 29,000 Moroccans responded to the regularization measure of 1991.

Visas became the chief means of controlling the flow. Without judging the way this instrument was applied or its effectiveness, immigration pressure is today not only under control but falling (Table 8).

Table 8. Visas granted 1991-1999

	Visas	% residence visas
1991	310,561	9.3
1992	368,488	5.24
1993	310,818	3.96
1994	444,905	3.52
1995	397,774	7.5
1996	374,412	10.07
1997	529,565	8.83
1998	660,359	14.13
1999	542,710	11.84

Source: Anuarios Estadísticos de Extranjería 1995-1999.

If we look at the percentages for Spain's closest southern neighbours, we see 108,424 visas were granted to North Africans in 1998 (16.4 per cent of the total), compared with 90,299 (22.7 per cent of the total) in 1995. Visas for Moroccans were 70.3 per cent of all visas for North Africans (62.3 per cent in 1995), followed by Algerians at 18.9 per cent (27.5 per cent 1995), Tunisians 4.7

pressure of immigration' and mentioned a survey that said 68 per cent of young Moroccans wanted to emigrate. This was a unnamed reference to a poll by the Casablanca weekly *Le Journal* (n° 18, 16-22 March 1998) that found 66.2 per cent of people between 20 and 29 who were asked said 'yes' to the question: 'If you could settle in a new country tomorrow to start a new life, would you do so?' This is not exactly the same as 'wanting to emigrate'. The survey involved 398 people over the age of 15, hardly a very credible sample.

[5] *Atlas de la inmigración magrebi en España,* edited by B. López García, compiled by A. Planet and A. Ramírez and published by the Autonomous University of Madrid and the Permanent Immigration Monitoring Centre, Madrid, 1996.

per cent (7.4 per cent), Mauritanians 4.8 per cent (2.6 per cent) and Libyans 1.3 per cent (0.2 per cent).

The figures were not very different in 1993 – 88,789 visas granted, 70 per cent of them to Moroccans. Visas for Latin Americans were far fewer, because not all the region's citizens need visas to enter Spain. In 1998, 55,830 visas were issued, against 24,599 in 1995. Cuba accounted for 23.6 per cent of the 1998 total for the region, Peru 22.2 per cent and the Dominican Republic 18.5 per cent. In 1995, Dominicans received 32 per cent and Peruvians 35 per cent, the countries with the largest number of applicants.

But the figures should be seen in a broader context. The total number of visas granted to North Africans and Latin Americans was 164,254 in 1998 (114,898 in 1995), but visas granted by Spanish consulates in Russia were 284,254 in 1998 (153,920 in 1995). However, we have no figures for 1995 and 1998 of how many visa applications were rejected, which would be useful to gauge immigration pressure. In 1993, 56,143 applications from North Africans were rejected, 53 per cent of them from Moroccans and 44.6 per cent from Algerians. Very probably most of the rejections were not of illegal residents, contrary to popular belief. One of the improvements in the short-lived 2000 aliens law was that officials had to say why a visa was refused and give the applicant a chance to appeal against the decision. But the government opposed these provisions and they were removed from the amended law.[6]

TEIM's analysis of visa applications made at the Spanish consulate in Tetuan between May 1991 and April 1993 are very revealing (Table 9). Of those rejected, 22.7 per cent were from company managers, civil servants and shopkeepers, and 23 per cent from students. Ten per cent of the rejections were from people who said they wanted to study, and of these 30.3 per cent were applicants below 25. Granting visas involves assessing the applicant's situation (age, profession, property, bank account, motives and documents) and being young and a student can mean someone trying to enter illegally. But to assert that all students who say they want to go to Spain to study, all women without a profession who say they want to go to visit a relative and all young people who want to be tourists are really intending to stay on in Spain illegally is going much too far.

[6] More openness about visa figures would be welcome. Compared with the ministries of the interior, labour and social affairs, the reluctance of Spanish consulates to give out information is quite striking.

Table 9. Tetuan consulate: visa applicants May 1991 – April 1993

- Profession and stated reasons for visit						
- Visa granted (%)						
	Tourism	**Business**	**Study**	**Joining Family**	**Visit to Family**	**Other**
Company managers/ civil servants	17.6	3.5	0.3	0	3.6	3.3
Shopkeepers	4.6	10.9	0	0	1.6	1.2
Workers	5.3	0.8	0	0.3	1	0.3
Students	4.5	0.5	4.8	0	1.3	0.6
Labourers/ domestic servants	3.3	2.1	0.2	0.8	0.3	0.7
No profession	8.6	0.2	0	1.6	3.0	1.3
Others/ retired people	4.9	1.9	0.2	0.3	1.3	1.2
Total	**48.8**	**19.9**	**5.5**	**3**	**14.1**	**8.6**
- Visas refused (%)						
Company managers/ civil servants	4	0.7	0.7	0	0.7	0.7
Shopkeepers	10.6	0.7	0	0	1.3	0
Workers	4.6	0	0	0	0.7	0
Students	9.9	0	9.3	0	0.7	0.7
Labourers/ domestic servants	8.6	0	0	0	4	0
No profession	7.3	0	0	2	9.9	5.3
Others/ retired people	7.3	0	0	0	0.7	1.4
Total	**52.3**	**1.4**	**10**	**2**	**18**	**8.1**

Table 9. Continued

- Age of applicants - Visa granted (%)					
	Under 25	**25-34**	**35-44**	**Over 45**	**% Total**
Company managers/ civil servants	0	10.9	9	8.7	28.6
Shopkeepers	0.2	6.9	5.4	6	18.5
Workers	0.3	4.1	2	0.9	7.3
Students	8.1	3.5	0	0	11.6
Labourers/ domestic servants	1.3	4.1	2.5	0.8	8.7
No profession	0.8	6.6	3.1	4.4	14.9
Others/ retired people	0.8	3.8	1.4	4.4	10.4
Total	**11.5**	**39.9**	**23.4**	**25.2**	**100**
- Visas refused (%)					
Company managers/ civil servants	0	2.7	2	1.3	6
Shopkeepers	2	11.3	1.4	2	16.7
Workers	3.4	2	0.7	0	6.1
Students	14.9	8.7	0	0	23.6
Labourers/ domestic servants	2.6	6	1.4	2.7	12.7
No profession	3.4	14.2	3.3	4	24.9
Others/ retired people	4	4	0.7	1.3	10
Total	**30.3**	**48.9**	**9.5**	**11.3**	**100**

Table 9. Continued

- Reasons for refusal (%)									
	(%) total	Did not qualify	Suspect	In excess of quota	No money	False doc'ts	Ex-illegal	Cand. w'd-raw	No case
Company managers/ civil servants	7	5.6	0	0.7	0.7	0	0	0	0
Shopkeepers	16.9	10.6	0	0	2.8	0	1.4	0.7	1.4
Workers	4.9	4.9	0	0	0	0	0	0	0
Students	24.7	20.5	1.4	0	0.7	0	0.7	0.7	0.7
Labourers/ domestic servants	13.3	11.2	0.7	0	1.4	0	0	0	0
No profession	23.3	20.5	1.4	0	0	0.7	0	0.7	0
Others/ retired people	9.9	8.4	0	0	1.5	0	0	0	0
Total	**100**	**81.7**	**3.5**	**0.7**	**7.1**	**0.7**	**2.1**	**2.1**	**2.1**

To measure immigrant pressure, we could also look at how many foreigners were turned back at the border and how many were detained aboard *pateras,* based on figures from the Dirección General de Política Interior. The *pateras* started to be a significant factor after the closure of the borders and introduction of visas in June 1991. Figures show the boats began appearing in 1992 but did not really starting coming until 1996, after which the number intercepted increased tenfold in two years. A total of 3,569 would-be illegal immigrants were picked up from such boats in 1999 and in 2000 (up to mid-December), the figure was 14,893. But the total number of people who managed to get into Spain in this or other illegal means is impossible to say. One interesting figure is the number of people escorted back to the border. In 1997, this included 22,230 Moroccans, 17,302 of whom did not manage to cross the Strait but were escorted out of the enclaves of Melilla (7,139) and Ceuta (10,163). Most of these in Spain itself were from the provinces of Cadiz (which includes Algeciras) (3,850), Almería (468) and Granada (684), all of them coastal provinces.

Table 10. Undocumented foreigners in Spain 1990-2000

	Turned back at border	Pateras intercepted	Arrested on pateras	Deported	Escorted to border
1990	73,959	–	–	4,733	959
1991	53,722	4	477	1,497	1,568
1992	15,030	15	616	971	2,131
1993	12,982	33	1,925	1,040	609
1994[1]	271,909	34	513	3,548	17,263
1995	173,988	130	1,257	3,398	12,833
1996	144,090	339	2,550	3,725	26,499
1997	5,865	399	887	4,071	23,209
1998	7,870	557	2,995	3,699	19,753
1999	8,946	475	3,569	3,734	16,928
2000	2,508[3]	780[2]	14,893[2]	639[3]	9,731[3]

Source: Dirección General de Política Interior.

1. Between 1994 and 1996, the criteria for recording data about people turned back at the border were changed.
2. Figures up to 14 December 2000.
3. Figures up to 30 June 2000.

The sharp increase in the number of *pateras* since 1991 might give a false impression. Before visas were introduced that year, future illegal immigrants had other ways of getting into Spain or passing through it en route to other EU countries. The media made a fuss about the appearance of just 15 *pateras* in the summer of 1992, yet the vastly greater number since 1995 has received less attention. So 'public sentiment' is subjective and largely depends on the size of newspaper headlines. There is no reason to play down a clearly dramatic trend, but when put in context it does not seem a major cause of the increased number of illegal immigrants.

Also, the above figures about intercepted *pateras* are only from monitoring the border with North Africa, specifically the Moroccan coast between Larache, Ued Lau and Tetuan. After 100 or so people drowned in the summer of 1992, this stretch was under tight surveillance for nearly two years, with a Moroccan policeman posted every 100 yards.

In a speech before their ambassadors on 10 February 1993, Morocco's King Hassan II called on the EU, the US, Canada, Japan and Sweden to give economical aid to develop the Rif area, the main source of illegal immigrants, and Morocco generally. At the time, the *pateras,* marijuana, alternative crops and the EU's negotiation of a free-trade agreement with Morocco were political issues. The police disappeared from the coast as soon as immigration was replaced by more prickly and urgent matters, such as fishing and the free-trade agreement.

The flow of immigrants and the monitoring of borders cannot be separated from Spain's relationship with its neighbours. In the book *Inmigración magrebi en España: El retorno de los Mariscos*,[7] immigration is described as a 'trading currency' in the history of Spanish-Moroccan relations. It was not a big issue when the book was written (1993), but the number of Moroccans in Spain has since increased – to become Morocco's second largest diaspora, after those in France – and is at the centre of relations between the two countries today.

Turning people back at the border is another issue concerning Morocco. False interpretation of the increased total number of foreigners turned back at Spain's borders (up from 12,982 in 1993 to 271,909 in 1994, due to new criteria for recording such data) could have led to wild speculation about the pressure of immigration. But there has been no such increased pressure. The town-enclaves of Ceuta and Melilla have a special status of frontier towns without customs officials and where the aliens law does not apply in the same way as in the rest of Spain and its islands. Each day, thousands of Moroccans without visas enter the towns from neighbouring provinces to do business of varying extent and legality. The impressive global figures include an average of 370 people a day being turned back from each town in 1994, 238 in 1995 and 197 in 1996, possibly people from more distant parts of Morocco looking for work. This is borne out by the fact that 95.6 per cent of those turned back at Spain's borders in 1994 were Moroccans, as were 97 per cent in 1995.

The figures about foreigners deported concern decisions to deport, only a fifth of which are actually carried out – between 3,000 and 4,000 a year between 1994 and 1999. This discrepancy shows immigrants took the risk of being expelled. The drop in deportations and people being escorted to the border in the first months of 2000 was due to the coming into effort of the new aliens law, which changed the criteria for carrying out these measures.

Sources of illegal immigration

The biggest fantasy immigration conjures up in host societies is about it being 'uncontrolled'. But immigration, including illegal entry, involves special aspects that have to be understood if it is to be controlled.

The *Atlas*[8] took a first look at the system of illegal immigration in Spain since 1991 by analysing the hidden regularization that the 1994 quota amounted to and in which nearly 8,000 Moroccans were regularized (Table 1). The *Atlas* looked at a sample of 10 per cent of those in each of the autonomous communities who were granted residence permits, so as to get a balanced view of the whole country. At first sight, about half the sample were similar to those regularized in 1991 as far as origin, age and gender were concerned. They also had passports issued before 1991 and were almost certainly immigrants who had been waiting to get

[7] *Inmigración magrebi en España: El retorno de los Moriscos*, edited by B. López García, Madrid, 1993.

[8] *Inmigración magrebi en España: El retorno de los Moriscos, op. cit.*

regularized. But the other half had a more varied profile and clearly contained new illegal immigrants who had arrived after 1991 (their passports had been issued later). Most of them (54 per cent) were in Andalusia.

The Moroccans in the 1994 quota included more women (16.4 per cent against 13.5 per cent in 1991) and were younger, but the most significant change was where they came from. The main home province was Oujda (28 per cent compared with 14 per cent in 1991). Provinces such as Nador, Al-Hoceima and Casablanca, which dominated the 1991 regularization, provided a lower percentage than before, as did Tetuan and Tangier, with about the same number of people as in 1991. But between 1991 and 1994, new provinces appeared in the figures, such as Beni-Mellal (8.3 per cent) and Taza (4 per cent), both double their 1991 score.

These are the new source areas of future illegal immigration (a significant part of emigration to Spain) because these provinces continue to send their people to Spain, as shown by the TEIM's surveys for the 2000 version of the *Atlas*, updating the 1996 edition.

A preliminary survey for the new *Atlas* looked at a 5 per cent sample of Moroccans who registered at their country's consulate in Algeciras between 1994 and the end of 1998. These were of Moroccans living in the regions of Andalusia, Murcia, Extremadura and Castilla-La Mancha (and excluding Gibraltar), including the most rural areas most dependent on illegal immigrant labour (Murcia and the Andalusian provinces of Almería and Huelva). Immigrants from Oujda and Beni-Mellal were still prominent among the newest arrivals. In Murcia, most of the 8,961 Moroccans granted residence in 1998 came from eastern Morocco. Oujda continued to provide more than half of all immigrants in the region, which had the fourth largest number of Moroccan immigrants, after Catalonia (49,124), Madrid (23,988) and Andalusia (20,438). Murcia also has an increasing number of immigrants from Beni-Mellal (18.7 per cent of its Moroccan immigrants in 1998, compared with 10 per cent in 1991).

In Almería, the Andalusian province where anti-foreigner riots erupted at El Ejido[9] in February 2000, there was a significant increase in Moroccans from the region of Tadla (Beni-Mellal) and Taza, while those from other parts of Morocco proportionally declined.

Another way of spotting the source areas of illegal immigration is to look at the people picked up on *pateras* coming from Morocco. The *Comisaría General de Extranjería y Documentación* provided a list of 794 illegal immigrants arrested in the first nine months of 1999 along the coasts of Algeciras, Almería and the Canaries, giving each person's place of origin. Again, most of these are in the provinces of Beni-Mellal, Oujda, Berkane, Nador and Ifni, with people from some places heading for the same parts of Spain (see Table 11).

[9] The European Civic Forum and the European Committee for the Defence of Refugees and Immigrants published a thorough report on the riots: *El Ejido. Terre sans loi. Rapport d'une commission internationale d'enquête sur les agressions racistes de février 2000 en Andalousie* (Bâle/Limans, 2000).

Table 11. Place of origin of those arrested aboard *pateras* in 1999 (%)

	Algeciras	Almería	Canaries
Beni Mellal	12.0	7.2	2.6
Berkane		20.4	
Casablanca	8.0		1.9
El Ayoun		0.5	6.4
El Kelaa	4.7	1.3	
Fez	3.2		
Gulimim			3.8
Ifni			43.6
Kenitra	8.0		
Larache	0.7		
Marrakesh	2.9	0.1	
Meknes	2.9	0.5	
Nador	1.1	43	
Tangier	7.6	0.3	
Tan Tan		0.3	13.4
Taza	4.7	0.5	0.6
Tetuan	0.7	0.3	2.6
Uxda	2.5	6.9	0.6
Others origins	31.1	15.5	15.2
Without precision	19.9	4.2	10.3
Total number of people	**276.0**	**362.0**	**156.0**

More than 40 per cent of those arrested were younger than 25 (47.4 per cent of those arriving in Almería, 44.8 per cent of those going to the Canaries and 44.2 per cent of those making for Algeciras) and nearly 40 per cent were between 26 and 35 (Canaries 46.1 per cent, Algeciras 45.6 per cent and Almería 37.5 per cent).

Debate about identity and the new aliens law

A front-page article in the French daily *Le Monde* on 14 October 1999 by Philippe Bernard headed 'Ceasefire over immigration' said France's obsession with immigration during the 1980s and 1990s, during which immigrants were used as scapegoats in various crises, had ended. Evidence of this was acceptance by former Prime Minister Alain Juppé and his conservative party that immigration was beneficial. Also, in the last parliamentary elections, won by a left-wing alliance, immigration was not the main issue for the first time in 20 years.

In Spain however, consensus among the political parties not to exploit immigration, achieved in 1991 on the eve of the first major regularization of foreigners, began to unravel in December 1999 with the ruling party's moves to prevent passage of the new aliens law. The issue of immigration seemed to enter the run-up to the 2000 parliamentary elections and this was confirmed by the shameful and dramatic events at El Ejido. The political consensus had broken down in the 1995 local elections in places with a large number of foreigners, but it was not until the parliamentary elections that immigration was shown to be a vote-catcher, because it had taken root in people's minds.

Spain is facing a debate about its identity, with some people, including respected figures such Miguel Herrero de Miñón, one of the authors of the 1978 national constitution, openly calling in the press for ethnic restrictions on immigration. In one article in 1999, headed 'They're Coming!'[10] he talked about the dangers of a society unsure of its identity, as in Austria, and of what might happen if Spaniards do not challenge certain taboos, especially concerning immigration. He said his own 'choice' was to base immigration firmly on 'linguistic and cultural affinity' or religious similarities and that Spain had the right to choose 'Ibero-Americans, Romanians and Slavs over than Africans'. He added that 'close cooperation with North Africa is one thing, but encouraging North African immigrants who are hard to absorb into Spanish society is quite another'.

The same stand was taken by the employers in El Ejido, who hired Eastern Europeans to break a strike there by Moroccans and also openly preferred 'dark people,' as they called immigrants from Sahel countries, over 'Moors' (North Africans, especially from Morocco). They saw the Sahelians as more obedient and less argumentative, in other words, more profitable and less likely to challenge the bosses' concept of progress.

The idea of some kind of ethnical 'filter' has been taken up by some of the media and more recently by some politicians. Federico Jiménez Losantos, a columnist for the daily paper ABC, has written that language, culture and religion should be taken into account when fashioning an 'easily assimilable' immigration. 'We are now in a position to choose who we allow in. If we don't, the immigrants will choose us, and then it'll be too late to object'.[11] Herrero de Miñón agrees in his article: 'Faced with the unimaginable "They're coming!" let's ask the calm question "Who are we going to let in?"'

Spain has not yet worked out the kind of immigration it wants and is hesitating between the French assimilation model and the British community-based one. The old 1985 aliens law, as Jordi Pujol, head of Catalonia's autonomous government, noted in a lecture he gave in Madrid on 4 July 2000 called 'The Challenge of Immigration,' was restrictive and reluctant to consider the rights of immigrants. The new, and of course temporary law that came into effect in February 2000[12] aimed more at socially absorbing immigrants, but it lacked clear

[10] *El Pais*, 9 October 1999.

[11] F. Jiménez Losantos, 'Faltan inmigrantes,' *ABC*, 25 February 1997. His article 'Inmigración racional,' in the same paper on 5 October 1999, was along the same lines.

[12] The law is discussed in issue 7 of the journal *Migraciónes,* put out by the University Immigration Research Institute, Madrid, June 2000. See especially articles by P. Charro Baena and J. M. Ruiz de Huidobro de Carlos, 'La Ley Organica 4/2000: Analisis tecnico-

principles because there is still no established Spanish system of dealing with immigration.

Instead, haste has produced the opposite and resulted in the new law. A calm debate about immigration has never taken place in Spain. The nearness of elections at the time of the parliamentary debate politicised the issue and broke the consensus when the law was adopted. Today the government has back-pedalled by amending the law to restrict the rights of undocumented foreigners – rights of assembly, association, belonging to a trade union and going on strike – even though the law is too new for its pros and cons to be judged properly.

This has put immigration back at the centre of a politically-charged debate about principles, a debate that lacks sober thought and a search for a specially-tailored model – things that are indispensable, since everyone seems to agree immigration will continue and is even necessary.

juridico de sus principales novedades,' pp. 7-56; J. .M. Ruiz de Huidobro de Carlos, 'La Ley Organica 4/2000: Historia de un desencuentro y razon de su desenfoque juridico,' pp. 57-88; and A. Alvárez Rodríguez, 'La nueva ley española de Extranjería: Ruptura e incumplimiento de Tampere? Innovación o seguimiento del modelo italiano?' pp. 89-136.

Chapter 4

Belgium's Regularization of Undocumented Aliens in 2000: Sign of a New Immigration Policy?

Marco Martiniello

Introduction

Belgium, like other European Union (EU) member-states such as France, Italy and Spain, recently began regularizing the situation of undocumented aliens within its borders. This move by the so-called 'rainbow' coalition government of Liberals, Socialists and Ecologists that has ruled the country since June 1999 caused a stir in the media. In Belgium, as in the rest of the EU, anything to do with immigration sets off much debate and causes tension in civil society and among politicians. The operation has shown how hard it is to get rid of the restrictive, security-oriented approach that immigration usually generates.

This chapter will try to place the regularization of undocumented aliens that began in January 2000 in the context of the wider debate (or absence of it) about a rigid immigration and asylum policy in Belgium and, by implication, within the EU.

First we will look at the historical background essential to a proper understanding of the 2000 regularization by going back to the country's first attempt at such an operation in 1974. Then we shall consider the 2000 operation, the way it was done, the issues it raised and the results of it up to 30 June 2000. Finally, we will discuss whether this latest operation is part of a shift, or even a clear change, in attitudes or policies about immigration in Belgium and the EU, or whether in fact it involves no significant change and simply entrenches the restrictive, security-oriented approach that prevails throughout the EU (Martiniello, 1992). The question mark in the title is no accident.

From one regularization to another: 1974 to 2000

On 1 August 1974, Belgium officially halted the entry of virtually all new immigrant workers (Martiniello and Rea 1997). The country was acting no differently from its EU partners. Faced with the first world oil crisis and a sharp rise in unemployment, most European countries that had hitherto made use of large numbers of foreign workers took similar steps. A few years later, some, including Belgium and France, even began encouraging immigrants to return to their home countries, though with little success (Weil 1995).

As it shut its borders to immigrants in 1974, Belgium carried out its first-ever large-scale regularization of undocumented aliens (Poncelet 1983: pp. 90-91). The country already had a lot of illegal foreign workers. Until then, the government had turned the immigration tap on when the economy was doing well and needing manpower and turned it off when the economy was in the doldrums (Martens 1976). This did not stop would-be immigrants – mainly Moroccans and Turks but also people from elsewhere in the EU – from entering Belgium on tourist visas and finding an 'illegal' job without much trouble.

Belgium's very powerful trade unions frowned upon what they saw as disloyal competition by illegal foreign workers with officially-documented workers, whether Belgian or immigrants. The illegal foreigners realised just as quickly that they were being more exploited than other workers. Ten illegal Moroccan immigrants began a hunger strike in a church in 1974 to try to obtain regularization and clear legal status as workers. The country's two big trade unions, the FGTB (the socialist and partly-communist Belgian General Labour Federation) and the CSC (Christian Trade Union Confederation) actively supported them because it was a golden opportunity to press for their major goal of equal conditions for all workers. They also wanted to get immigrants more involved in union activities.

The government considered basing regularization on whether a person could show proof of residence in the country and then proof of having a job. Since the candidates were both undocumented and illegal, this was impossible. The unions reacted swiftly and the government agreed to accept simply verbal proof of residence (from a witness, for example). In all, 7,000 undocumented foreign workers (90 per cent of those who applied) were given residence and labour permits.

So, Belgium's immigration policy in the mid-1970s was based on a halt to all new worker immigration, incentives to return to the country of origin and regularization of foreign workers. Those who could not get documents were deported.

It would take too long to describe how immigration and asylum policy have changed since then.[1] But it was clear the ban on all new immigrant workers could not be fully enforced. Martens, cited by Groenendijk and Hampsink (1995: 11), says that about 100,000 new work permits were issued between 1975 and 1985. More than 33,000 went to new immigrants and the rest to foreigners arriving mainly as relatives of immigrants already there.

Jobs made possible by separate agreements between Belgium and other countries were no longer the preferred way in for would-be immigrants. Joining family members, studying in Belgium and, later on requests for asylum, along with

[1] See collectif, *La Belgique et ses immigrés. Les politiques manquées,* Brussels, De Boeck University, 1997.

illegal entry into the country organised by racketeers were the main forms of immigration after the 1974 official shutdown.

With the collapse of the Berlin Wall, Belgium and its European partners were hit by the rapid spread of the asylum crisis. The harshness of Belgium's policy was shown by the fact that only five per cent of asylum-seekers obtained the coveted status of refugee. Many rejected applicants went underground, while others were deported. Some tried again in other countries but found it just as hard because a joint EU policy on asylum was emerging. Some sectors of the Belgian economy (Horeca, construction, textiles and agriculture) were looking for cheap and obedient workers, so undocumented illegal workers found jobs which, if far from ideal, were at least better than those from where they had come. The number of foreigners living in Belgium without any documents or with invalid ones may well have increased during the 1980s and 1990s, but there are virtually no reliable figures to back this up.

Throughout the 1990s, the Belgian authorities regularized very few immigrants – each year between a few hundred and just over 1,000 – and processed them one by one. The idea of a large-scale regularization that caught on among NGOs and community groups sparked little interest within the federal government.

On 22 September 1998, as Belgium was going through one of the most turbulent periods of its history with a spectacular string of scandals and human dramas, Semira Adamu, a young Nigerian woman whose asylum request had been turned down, died of suffocation while she was being deported by police. Her death forced the Socialist Interior Minister, Louis Tobback, a Fleming, to resign and focused Belgians' attention on the dramatic plight of many undocumented aliens. A broad political and public debate ensued, stoked by a campaign by illegal immigrants who occupied churches and staged hunger strikes to demand regularization. The campaign by them and on their behalf spilled beyond the confines of leftist and humanitarian circles and took on a national, even transnational dimension.

Madjiguène Cissé, one of the movement's spokespersons in France, visited Belgium many times. After a determined year-long battle, both inside and outside parliament and the government, the new administration that emerged from the June 1999 elections partly yielded to the campaigners by including regularization in a 'new' approach to immigration outlined in its policy statement. That policy was based on three closely-linked elements – a 'realistic and humane' asylum policy, a stepped-up fight against racism and other kinds of intolerance and the social integration of immigrants and their children.[2]

[2] 'The way forward to the 21st Century', a draft agreement among the federal majority that was supported by the Socialists, Liberals and Ecologists, 8 July 1999.

The 2000 regularization campaign

To carry out regularzation as fast as possible, the Liberal Interior Minister Antoine Duquesne, a Walloon, decided to use the legal instrument of a royal decree.[3] This was fiercely criticised by one opposition party in parliament, the racist Flemish nationalist Vlaams Blok, which said it effectively amended the 1980 law about the entry, visits, domicile and removal of foreigners.[4] In Belgium, an act of parliament takes precedence over a royal decree, which cannot alter or water down a law. The Blok appealed to the State Council, which said it was right. The party's action was predictable because it wins votes by opposing immigration and integration. As soon as a pro-immigration measure is taken, it launches a political or legal campaign to obstruct it.

This political dispute and procedural hijacking forced the majority in parliament to come up with a law permitting regularization, though at a slower and more cumbersome pace than the royal decree. The law, allowing regularization of certain categories of immigrants in the country, was passed on 22 December 1999 and published in the official gazette on 10 January 2000. The first phase of the operation could begin. Candidates for regularization had just three weeks from 10 January to file applications with officials of the town where they lived.

Starting on 10 January, the Belgian government restored checks along its borders, having asked its European partners for a temporary waiver of the Schengen Agreement that does away with border controls inside the area formed by the signatory states. Gendarmes were sent to man border posts and vehicles entering the country were thoroughly searched to prevent an influx of immigrants seeking to take advantage of the regularization. The Interior Minister said he feared people-smugglers would step up their activities, by promising their immigrant clients legal status in Belgium.

But the precautions were mostly to show Belgians that regularization did not mean the door had been completely opened to immigrants. In fact, it did not basically change Belgium's restrictive immigration policy and this was the message conveyed through the media by the Interior Minister, who visited several border crossing points. As if to emphasize that a strict policy was still in force, the government resumed deporting foreigners, except those who applied for regularization. Its declared aim was a short-term, once-and-for-all operation regularizing a large number of undocumented aliens case by case according to clear criteria (Carlier 1999), instead of the hitherto very small number each year.

The law applies to foreigners living in Belgium on 1 October 1999. Those who arrived afterwards cannot apply for regularization under any circumstances. The law stipulates four categories of people who can be regularized (article 2).

[3] The royal decree of 6 October 1999 set the criteria for applying for regularization of residence status without having to cite special circumstances listed in Article 9, § 3, law of 15 December 1980 on the entry, visits, domicile and removal of foreigners. (*Moniteur Belge,* 7 October 1999).

[4] The law of 15 December 1980 (*Moniteur Belge,* 31 December 1980) was amended several times between 1984 and 1998 and is the basis of Belgian immigration policy.

First, asylum-seekers caught up in an overly-long procedure who have not received a decision on their application after four years, or three years in the case of families with children who are minors. Second, those who have no real possibility of returning to their countries because of war, for example. Third, fragmented sentence seriously ill people. And fourth, those who have put down lasting roots in the country by living there for at least six years without having received a deportation order in the previous five years. These are people considered in effect 'assimilated'. In their applications, foreigners can cite one or more of the four categories. The law excludes regularization of those deemed a serious threat to public order and national security (article 5).

Undocumented aliens and NGOs supporting them criticized the arbitrary nature of the criteria. How do you define a serious illness? What exactly are the circumstances beyond a foreigner's control that prevent return to the country of origin? How do you define lasting roots in Belgium? Interior Ministry documents give no clear answers, so the risk of arbitrariness remains. The criteria were not, however, re-worded.

Regularization includes the right to unrestricted residence and to social security benefits in Belgium. At first, the right to work was not mentioned. At the insistence of the federal Labour Minister, the Walloon Socialist Laurette Onkelinckx, those regularized were given an indefinite work permit, which seems very logical. Granting a residence permit with no right to work would simply make a former undocumented alien dependent on public funds. Unregularized foreigners were to be deported, the Interior Minister said.

At the end of the first three-week phase of the regularization operation, 36,000 applications had been made, representing about 50,000 people, including 23,000 minors. Two nationalities stood out – Congolese (17.6 per cent) and Moroccans (12.4 per cent) – among the 140 nationalities who applied.[5] The numbers were seen as quite high but there was no indication that all potential candidates had applied. They also do not show how many illegal undocumented aliens there are who would not qualify for regularization.

Under the law, applications are handled by a special commission made up of eight tribunals, each comprising a lawyer, a judge and a representative of an NGO working with illegal foreigners (article 3). The commission has a staff of civil servants from the Aliens Office who check that the applications are complete and sort out the ones likely to be approved by the Minister of the Interior. Incomplete ones are sent straight to the Minister, with a note advising their rejection. If the Minister disagrees, the application is sent back to the commission, which has one of the tribunals hear the case. Complete applications that nevertheless have problems, such as attached documents of suspicious origin and not obviously meeting any of the four criteria, go directly to the tribunals, who make a recommendation to the Minister. Complete applications with no problems are sent straight to the Minister who can, again, if he disagrees with the commission's suggestion for approval, still send them back for review by a

[5] This data, taken from an article by M. Vandemeulebroucke in the daily newspaper *Le Soir* of 2 March 2000, is provided reluctantly by the Ministry of the Interior.

tribunal. Because of the large number of applications and the fairly cumbersome procedure, many predicted that the regularization operation would take a long time.

Between the deadline for filing applications and early summer 2000, argument and discussion arose about the slowness of processing them and taking a decision, about the arbitrariness involved in the procedure and about the living conditions of the applicants.

One controversy was about access to jobs and social security benefits for applicants while their cases were being considered. The jobs question was answered by a federal Labour Ministry circular allowing them to work during this period.[6] This was partly because applicants for regularization seemed to lose the right to social security benefits, except emergency medical treatment. Not allowing them to work would have been casting them out with no resources or forcing them into the black economy.

More heated argument occurred over a proposed temporary right to social security benefits. Many applicants were refused benefits or cut off by public social assistance centres (CPAS) in the towns and villages where they lived. Often through lawyers working with undocumented immigrant groups, they took legal action against what they saw as blatantly unjust. Labour courts in a number of towns, such as Liège (22 March 2000), Verviers (16 April) and Brussels (8 June), ruled in their favour, saying that since they were allowed to stay in the country during their application, they should also have the right to social security benefits. The Walloon Socialist MP and chairman of the central Brussels CPAS, Yvan Mayeur, presented a bill giving them that right. It stirred up controversy among the ruling coalition even before it was considered by the lower house of parliament's health committee. The Liberals and the Flemish Socialists were most opposed. They said it would be dangerous to appear to give advantages to foreigners only a few months before the October 2000 local elections, in which the racist Vlaams Blok was taking part.

Another hot issue was the creation and composition of the regularization commission itself and the functions and impartiality of its staff. It was set up, well behind schedule, on 8 May 2000. The delay was partly because, although officially independent, all kinds of political and linguistic balances had to be maintained in its composition. The Minister of the Interior was also busy wrestling with a tricky reform in the police and with huge security problems involved in holding European Cup football matches in Belgium and the Netherlands in June 2000, and so was perhaps forced to give lower priority to the second stage of regularization.

Once the commission was set up, problems arose between the staff and the tribunals because of the very slow processing of the applications. The daily newspaper *Le Soir* wrote in June that, at the current rate, the whole operation would take eight years.[7] By the beginning of June, only three applications involving seven people had been approved and there was no sign of things being substantially speeded up. The approach of local elections on 8 October and the political majority's fear of new advances by the Vlaams Blok in towns in Flanders

[6] Circular of 6 April 2000, published in *MoniteurBelge* of 19 April 2000.
[7] *Le Soir,* 16 June 2000, p. 11.

perhaps had something to do with it, unfortunately for the applicants who were left in suspense and anguish about whether they would be rejected and deported.

Towards a new immigration policy?

The regularization campaign begun by Minister of the Interior Duquesne was not just needed, it was essential. Political agreement on a realistic and humane asylum policy emerged inside the coalition government in summer 1999 and the Minister of the Interior really only implemented it. As far as principles go, a democratic society cannot allow for the physical presence of people without any legal status, that is, without substantial rights and without real obligations. Such legal non-existence and lack of status, along with poverty, makes undocumented aliens major targets of all kinds of economic exploitation and racism as well as forcing them to live in the barely-legal informal economy to survive.

The situation is all the more intolerable because of the state's failure to process the asylum applications and because it involves a large number of children (23,000 applications for regularization include one or more minors). The time between filing an application and getting a decision is often far too long. During this time, many applicants have settled in Belgium, had children and, some would say, have become part of the society. How can the authorities morally justify deporting people whose applications they have taken sometimes more than five years to turn down? Do children who were born in Belgium or arrived there very young not have a right to protection from the state?

The regularization operation is definitely a partial response to these questions. The government's goodwill and good intentions made the first phase of it a success. But the whole operation seems quite inadequate in the context of the larger issues raised by the flow of immigrants at the start of the third millennium, which will probably be notable for population mobility. The political, economic, environmental and demographic reasons for people moving around are not going to disappear. Belgium, like its European partners, will remain a country that draws immigrants. Beyond a firm and humane asylum policy, of which the once-off regularization operation is part, is it not time to start a debate in Belgium and the rest of Europe about drawing up a clear immigration policy as called for in the Amsterdam Treaty?

Globalization of the economy means more immigration to rich countries. For the past few years, the OECD, the ILO and the European Commission have stressed the futility of the notion and the talk of 'zero immigration' by some countries, including Belgium. Other EU member-states have already moved on. Italy has introduced an annual quota system for immigrants based on unemployment levels, so that those allowed in are mainly the ones likely to find work. Germany recently allotted 30,000 work permits to alleviate the serious shortage of computer industry workers it has. Many of these new immigrants will come from India. In Belgium too, despite high unemployment, some parts of the economy are short of skilled and specialized workers, and employers would not object to easing immigration curbs to fill these jobs. A recent United Nations study says immigration could also help solve the problem of Europe's ageing population.[8]

The European Union seems to have no choice. It has to accept itself as a continent of immigrants and draw up immigration and asylum policies which take account of its humanitarian obligations, along with its broad economic interests and those of its members but also those of the immigrants' countries of origin. However beneficial Belgium's regularization operation is, it cannot meet the enormous challenge that calls for a profound change of mentalities in Belgium and Europe.

Perhaps the Belgian operation has set off a usefull democratic debate that is very difficult in a country with a solid and well-organized political extreme-right, but it seems to be making headway. The Brussels Socialist senator Mohamed Daïf has called zero immigration 'an illusion we shouldn't think about any more'.[9] A headline in the weekly magazine *LeVif/L'Express* in April 2000 asked: 'Should we reopen our frontiers to immigrants?'[10] The federal budget and social integration Minister, the Flemish Socialist Johan Vandelanotte, has said it would be better to tackle the discrimination preventing 'aliens'[11] from finding work than to bring in more[12]. The distance between these points of view still seems enormous but perhaps another taboo is about to be re-examined in Belgium alongside the regularization operation. We can only hope so.

References

Carlier, J.-Y. (1999), 'Pour une politique migratoire humaine et réaliste en Belgique, dans l'Europe de demain,' *Annales de Droit de Louvain*, vol. 59, n°3, pp.1-24.

Groenendijk, K. and Hampsink, R. (1995), *Temporary Employment of Migrants in Europe*, Nijmegen: Catholic University, Reeks Recht en Samenleving.

Martens, A. (1976), *Les Immigrés. Flux et reflux d'une main d'œuvre d'appoint*, Louvain: EVO/Louvain University Press.

Martiniello, M. (1992), 'L'immigration : menace pour l'État-Nation ou révélateur de son caractère obsolète?', *Revue Suisse de Sociologie*, 18: 3, pp. 657-673.

Martiniello, M. and Rea A. (1997), 'Construction européenne et politique d'immigration,' in Collectif, *La Belgique et ses immigrés. Les politiques manquées*, Brussels: De Boeck University, pp. 121-143.

Poncelet, M. (1983), *Analyse des attitudes syndicales envers le phénomène de l'immigration en Belgique (FGTB-CSC)*, thesis for degree in sociology, Liège University.

[8] *Replacement Migration. Is it A Solution to Declining and Ageing Populations?* Population Division, Department of Economic and Social Affairs, United Nations Secretariat, New York, 21 March 2000.

[9] Speaking as a guest on RTBf's *Matin Première* programme on 11 April 2000.

[10] Le Vif/L'Express, no. 2548, 5-11 May 2000.

[11] A term used especially in Flanders to describe immigrant Belgians of foreign origin.

[12] Speaking at the end of a conference on racism at Ghent University (10-12 April 2000).

Population Division, Department of Economic and Social Affairs, United Nations Secretariat (2000), *Replacement Migration. Is it A Solution to Declining and Ageing Populations?* New York: United Nations.

Weil, P. (1995), *La France et ses étrangers*, Paris: Folio-Actuel.

Population Division, Department of Economic and Social Affairs, [illegible]
Secretariat [illegible]
[illegible]
[illegible]

Chapter 5

European Citizenship and Migration

Catherine Wihtol de Wenden

Introduction

After the Risorgimento, Massimo d'Azeglio declared: 'We have made Italy, now we have to do the Italians'. Nowadays, we could say that once we have built the European Union, we have to make the Europeans. Since the Maastricht Treaty on European Union of 1992, in its article 8, Europe has decided to give birth to citizens. But European citizenship still seems to remain far from the nationals of nation-states, because it is not defined by a people, a territory with fixed borders, nor a common language and history or by a consensual culture. Moreover in its practice, it includes democratic shortages which delay the effectiveness of a full citizenship. The lack of symbols of 'affectio societatis' give way to the reign of experts as well as to the development of a sad and grey citizenship. This difficulty in defining itself and in living takes its roots from the conflictual history between Europe and citizenship, illustrated by three founding paradoxes. The first paradox lies in the fact that modern citizenship has been built against it, i.e. Europe of monarchies and great empires have had to face with newly born nation-states. A second paradox of European citizenship is that it proceeds from some distantiation towards nation, while nation-states and citizenship were forming before a couple of rivals and associates:[1] thus the idea of a European supra-nationality seems to create a spontaneous misunderstanding, restoring old fears. The third paradox is that European citizenship challenges many classical definitions of citizenship founded on a mutual obligation between the citizen and the state. When there is no state, is it possible to imagine the exercise of citizenship with some rights, but few visible duties and with references to populations, cultures and territories in a constant evolution?

However, Europe has decided to become the heart of a renewed citizenship with the Maastricht Treaty of 1992 founding the political Union, in its article 8; although in search of itself for lack of symbolic imaginaries, European citizenship represents a big project; it means a dissociation between nationality and citizenship, a constitutional innovation. It supposes the elaboration of a common culture beyond national borders after centuries of conflicts as well as the definition of new civic values ignored by the founding civic values included in the declaration of human rights of 1789.

[1] C. Wihtol de Wenden, 'Nation et citoyenneté/un couple d'associés-rivaux,' *Nations et nationalismes*, Paris, La Découverte, 1996, pp.49-60.

The European project was first formalised by the economy and freedom of trade (CECA, Communauté européenne du charbon et de l'acier, 1954, Euratom and common market in the Treaty of Rome 1957) and then enlarged from six members (France, Germany, Italy, Benelux) to nine (Denmark, Ireland, United Kingdom, 1972), then ten (Greece) , twelve (Spain and Portugal 1986) and fifteen (Austria, Sweden, Finland, 1995), in parallel with a more political dimension (election of the European Parliament by universal suffrage 1975, Single European Act 1985, Maastricht 1992, Amsterdam 1997, Euro 1999).

But the European citizen feels very far from this process, which is helped by the attachment of states to the exercise of their sovereignty in fields such as border control, nationality and right of asylum and by the rise of regionalism and the reign of experts. To them, Europe may look like a club, sharing a mininum of common values (liberalism, free trade, individualism, democracy, secularism, reconciliation between France and Germany, East and West) around an 'unidentified political object', as says Jacques Delors.

European citizenship looks like citizenship in the antique Rome, with series of concentric circles, a dynamic of center/periphery, middle classes/excluded in a neo-tourainian approach around a civility made of urban values ('urbanité' and 'civilité'). The Europe of citizens follows the Europe of workers decided in 1968. A dynamization of the political content will not be made without a very strong political will, because it cannot be decided only by a treaty.

In the context of an evolutive political Europe, European citizenship has to cope with immigration. Among the various factors which contribute to the framework and conceptualization of European citizenship, immigration plays an important part, but with some limits. This paper will focus on the impact of immigration on the content of European citizenship, as well as on the limits brought by European citizenship on the condition of extra-Europeans.

Defining European citizenship

In his introduction to Antye Wiener's book on *European Citizenship Practice,*[2] Charles Tilly says: 'Citizenship grew up as a feature of strong, centralized States, yet to day the European Union's form of citizenship attaches its members to an institution that is not a state and may well undermine states as Europe has hitherto known them'.

Compared with Jean Bodin's definition of national citizenship (a mutual obligation between the citizen and the state), European citizenship cannot be defined by the classical attributes of citizenship: the nation-state has lost its monopoly of references, challenging the former relations between nationality and citizenship. It is an evolutive citizenship in an evolutive territory with non-fixed member states, populations and cultures, beyond the national framework, highly challenged by immigration.

[2] A. Wiener, *European Citizenship Practice*, Westview Press, 1997.

Citizenship and Europe: a couple of rivals and associates

If Europe of the great empires and monarchies has been questioned in the past, by citizenship as a new invention of peoples to challenge the 'European concert,' citizenship is also presently challenged by Europe, because European citizenship refers to other relations than between the citizen and the nation-state.

Nation Nation was first associated with citizenship. Before that nationalism did not oppose citizenship. At the end of the 18th Century and well into the 19th, nation and citizenship seemed complimentary, before dissociating themselves at the end of the 19th and into the 20th Century. It is acceptable to think that the modern concept of the nation was born at Valmy, September 20, 1792, when France defeated the Prussians to the cry of 'vive la Nation':[3] the armed nation symbolized at that time the defense of citizenship and the affirmation of national sovereignty. In 1848, the movement of nationalities, which would notably shake Italy and Austria-Hungary was equally bound to the quest of citizenship and emancipation. It was not until the end of the 19th Century that the idea of nation came, particularly in France, divided between a popular nationalism, defined by Michelet and illustrated by the Commune of 1871 and anti-parliamentary nationalism, protectionist even xenophobic, with a regionalist tendency (Barres) and an elitist and conservative tendency (Maurras) after the defeat of 1870. In 1882, the celebrated definition of Ernest Renan (*Qu'est-ce qu'une Nation?)* decided with this break between nation and citizenship because it proposed in a revisited social contract, a century after 1789, an osmosis between the citizenship and the nation 'The nation is a soul, a spiritual principle, a will to live together,' and its existence is a plebiscite of all the days. The republican school of Jules Ferry also contributed to this fusion between nation and citizenship broken afterwards by l'Action Française and the Vichy Regime. Today the distinction between nationality and citizenship seems commensurate with the citizenship based on residence locale, dissociated from nationality, European citizenship, and the rising of micro and macro-nationalism with ethnic purification to the east and national preference (les Français 'de souche') or region (Italy, Belgium) to the west.

Citizenship Initially defined as the resident of a city (according to the Académie française dictionary of 1694), the citizen was afterwards identified by the social contract within the framework of the state, before being bound to the nation (le petit Larousse defined the citizen as the member of a state, considered from the point of view of his rights and political obligations). In France, citizenship preceded nationality: as prescribed in *La Déclaration des droits de l'Homme et du citoyen* of 1789 it covers a space more vague and more dynamic than nationality, prescribed in the civil code. Rather than a right, citizenship would be then a quality, even of capacities, written in variable geometry, local, region, nation state, Europe, the world. Some have added to it enterprise or environment, but with these conclusions, often tied to nationality (thus, reciprocal citizenship between

[3] 'Long live the Nation'.

Europeans of the European Union at the level of local political rights which excludes those residents outside the community, because the European Union can create a citizenship but it cannot grant a nationality).

Sometimes in crisis, threatened by membership to a different community which takes precedent, ethnic or religious or, on the contrary, by the excess of individualism (the spirit of security) it survives in spite of everything just as well, compared to other alliances: the citizen was not ousted by the comrade neither by the consumer nor the user. One can also ask if the citizenship agrees right away, or if it is gained, with the conditions (the most essential being nationality) which evolved in time. In 1789, the priest Siéyès (*Qu'est-ce que le Tiers Etat ?),*[4] distinguished between active and passive citizens and, lasting close to a century, citizenship, when it existed, was, in France, masculine and censored until 1848. Other capacities also evolved: the age of the majority, went from 21 to 18 years of age in 1974, the indignation by decision of justice, the practice of certain professions (military under the Third Republic), sex (women did not acquire the right to vote until 1944), nationality itself did not always confer the full exercise of citizenship (case of the second poll of colonial Algeria). Thus there existed nationals who were not citizens. Inversely, there was also the case of citizenship without nationality.

During the French Revolution the question of nationality was not posed: the revolutionary logic elevated the position of citizens to 'good' foreigners and pronounced foreigners 'bad' citizens. The constitution of 1793 accorded citizenship to those who proved civic and loyal spirit with regard to the revolution. The Commune of 1871 also defined as citizens those stangers who engaged in the struggle. A century later, during the 1980', the theme of the new citizenship, developed notably by the French-Arab movement, looked to resume with this tradition, which disassociates nationality and citizenship being founded by this at the local level, by residence and concrete participation in city affairs, independent of nationality. European citizenship established by the Treaty of Maastricht, founded on the reciprocity of rights between Europeans of the Union, opens a constitutional breach in the practice of sovereignty yesterday reserved for exclusively nationals in matters of local elections.

Other examples of the local right to vote accorded to foreigners, generally those outside of the community, since the middle of the 1970s (Sweden, Denmark, Netherlands, Norway) offer other examples of disassociation between citizenship and nationality. Moreover, the appearance of newly excluded individuals from citizenship who are often nationals, suggests citizenship does not happen right away; it would be then tied to a sort of urban civility western with, at the margin, populations lacking the socio-politicalties or, for other members, community order, are only significant. One is not born a citizen, one becomes one, said the Condorcet, by the instruction or, as one would say today, information. Even though one does not generally choose his nationality (except in the case of naturalization and voluntary acquisition of the nationality), the citizenship does not decide: it is related to brotherhood, while liberty and equality are rights.

[4] *What is the Third State ?*

Inseparable from political and democratic reference, maintaining the ties of skittish cohabitation with the nation, it is today threatened by the excess of individualism (the spirit of security), by the tribalistic identity, and by world-wide ultraliberal consumerism (the world of networks).

European citizenship has ceased to be linked with national idioms. Because of the paradoxes of its birth, it is in search of its content, with a deficit of symbols. This content has to be looked for beyond the nation-states, with some rewriting of common and consensual history and more festivity.

Framing European citizenship

European citizenship has three characteristics: it is a citizenship of attribution, a citizenship of reciprocity and a hierarchised citizenship.

A citizenship of attribution Europe cannot give a nationality and it is the nation-state which confers to its nationals the status of European citizens, like an added 'étiquette'. This specificity introduces some discrepancies in the implementation of the attributes of European citizenship around the question: who is an European? This question is all the more accurate as the fact of being or not a European has consequences on rights inside Europe (namely freedom of circulation and political rights). In recent years, immigration has raised the question of the inadequacies between access to nationality in immigration countries according to their philosophies of rights (of the soil, of the blood or mix). The game is not the same for all: each country has its own definition of who is a national, of who is a European. It depends on its history, its colonial past, its geography, its neighbourhood, its geopolitical strategies. The consequences are heavy in terms of identification of internal border towards the 'other'.

A citizenship of reciprocity, highly hierarchized European citizenship is a hierarchized one, built on a series of concentric circles, 'à la romaine'. At the center we find the national of the state where he is living, then the European whose rights are reciprocal with those given to European foreigners in other European states, then the long term non-European residents, then the non-European non residents, the refugees, and, at the margins, the asylum seekers and the illegals. For Europeans, the rule is almost the same for all, but in each European state, the border between Europeans and extra-Europeans varies, introducing a new institutional border in substitution to the former territorial border with some trouble hierarchizations around colour, religion or former colonial status. Facing this new trend, the immigrant motto 'citizenship of residence' has lost none of its strength and legitimacy with the implementation of the rights of European citizenship. For those who have been living in Europe for more than twenty years as immigrant workers, having sometimes benefited from the freedom of circulation in colonial pasts, European citizenship is a regression, juridically and politically speaking, because it cancels several years of civic mobilisation around a legitimacy of stay based on work and residence.

Some rights, but few duties Article 8 of the Maastricht Treaty defines the right of Europeans: freedom of circulation, of work and settlement in Europe, right to vote and to be elected at the European Parliament, local political rights, right to appeal to the European Court of Justice against one's state, right of petition, right to address to the Mediator, right to be represented diplomatically by a European state in a third country when one's country is not represented. However, there remain some disparities due to particular relations between former colonial countries having bilateral links with their former colonies (France/Algeria, Portugal/PALOP – countries with original Portuguese idiom). Moreover, European citizenship cannot be opposed to extra-European nation-states as such: among the list of countries exempted from visas of entrance by the United States, which was established in 1997, most European countries are among them but not all: nationals of Portugal and Greece must hold visas to enter in the U.S.

Among all these rights, the freedom of circulation, settlement and work all over Europe is the most important. It existed before Maastricht (with the Schengen agreement of 1985, the uniform European passport of 1985 and the effectivness of internal borders of 1992). It supposed that the internal mobility of Europeans would be quantitatively much more important than for extra-Europeans across external borders, which has been in the fact exactly the reverse. It is Germany (1.7 million), France (1.3 million) and the United Kingdom (768,000) which welcome most Europeans from other countries: a migration of educated people more than of workers. By reinforcing the external borders and opening the internal ones, Europe is contradicting the trends of migration flows. Since 1991, this suppression of visas has been extended to Visegrad countries (Poland, Czeck Republic, Hungary) and then to all PECO's (Bulgary in 2000 and Romania in 2001). As for political rights, they are founded on the reciprocity of rights: with Europe, citizenship is no more the expression of national sovereignty and the border is now inside Europe, between Europeans and extra-Europeans. Voting rights include the participation and eligibility of Europeans to the election of the European Parliament since 1979 and local voting rights in the country of residence. But it is limited to Europeans, excluding the long term non-European residents (in spite of the associations' mobilisation and the Vetter Report of 1989). Some disparities of representation nevertheless exist between European countries: in Italy, less than 1 per cent of the vote elects an M.P. against 20 per cent in the U.K. to give a seat to a party. It is the nature of the election (managerial or political) which defines the quality of the territory, local or national. All European countries have changed their constitution in order to put it in accordance with this dissociation between nationality and citizenship and to change the definition of sovereignty.

This opens a juridical possibility for granting local political rights to all foreigners. But one can also argue that, due to the delay of implementation of this clause to Europeans (in France, at the local elections of 1995, 1,5 million of Europeans have not been able to exert their civic rights, due to a lack of information), the extension of such rights to extra-Europeans in countries that have not yet done it, will be delayed for a long time as will the debate on this question (Sweden in 1975, Denmark in 1981, the Netherlands in 1985 have not waited for

Europe to grant local political rights to all their long-term resident foreigners). The other rights of citizenship are: diplomatic protection, right of petition and of appeal to the mediator. The social rights are the weak point of European citizenship: lack of solidarity inside the Union, strong disparities of salaries, welfare and other allocations, which introduce inequalities of membership in spite of successes: possibility to study, to acquire diplomas and to exert civil services (except for functions implying the exercise of national sovereignty) everywhere in Europe. As for cultural rights, they are conditioned by the revisiting of a common history (a history not only made of conflicts and wars) by more visibility of European symbols and by more festivity (the hymn of Beethoven, the feast on 9 May and the flag - the Virgin surrounded with the twelve apostles, the twelve golden stars on dark blue - having nothing to do with the strong collective imaginaries carried on by the national feasts and their symbols of belonging). We lack a European civic teaching, of 'lieux de mémoire' (memory places), of historical representation for common imaginaries. General conceptions of European citizenship coexist: a citizenship founded on the 'living together,' legitimized by residence and new citizenship (effective participation), a citizenship founded on the social contract revisited, a citizenship founded on reciprocal rights between E.U. citizens. But 40 years is a short period in which to build a European 'affectio societatis,' compared with centuries of wars and conflicts: European citizenship is an added identity to the national one, putting in common some minimum cultural pasts: Greece and Rome, Christianisty, Renaissance, Enlightenment, Reason, Socialism, Liberalism, Colonialism, Industrial Revolution, Democracy and Welfare, Secularism.

The cultural unity of Europe may today be achieved against the representation of the other as the extra-Europeans, the colonized, the coloured, the Muslims if stronger feelings of membership are not created to counter the 'grey' literature of Brussels. The democratic deficit of European citizenship also partially lies in the absence of commitment requested from its members: many of the former symbols of belonging to a political community have disappeared: military service, direct taxes, representation by a parliament invested of a legislative power, a common education, proximity of institutions and transparency of the decision-making process. Moreover, unlike many others, European citizenship has not been built after a battle with identified enemies, but on peace and market. Its symbolic border profiles around immigration and Islam, and it becomes difficult to say if identity defines the territory of Europe or if the territory defines its identity (the inclusion of Greece, the exclusion of Turkey and the pending question around the application of Morocco or the so-called 'Maastricht's criteria' asked to eastern European states are interesting). But the European Union makes it possible to think about a citizenship beyond the nation-state, with new values not included in the Declaration of 1789: anti-racism, protection of environment, extra-national solidarities, humanitarian concepts.

The impact of immigration on European citizenship: Contributions and limits

Contributions

Extra-European immigration has brought three main fields to European citizenship in progress: a juridical approach, dissociating nationality from citizenship and focusing on the discrepancies due to the various regimes of nationality codes all over Europe, a cultural content bringing multiculturalism to the center of the debate and a civic insight for new values around: can one be European with other loyalties?

The juridical contribution By putting on the political and constitutional table the debate on the 'new citizenship:' a citizenship legitimized by residence, focused on participation to 'here and now,' independent from nationality, civic associationism, namely in France, has introduced and developed the theme of dissociation between nationality (depending on the law) and citizenship (the effectiveness of participation in the city). Some '*beur*' (franco-maghrebian) associations, such as Texture with Saïd Bouamama have gone rather far in the theorization of the divorce between these two notions in 1989.[5] Their claims were preceded before by the mobilization for local political rights in the second part of the 1970s, headed namely by the FASTI (Fédération des Associations de soutien aux travailleurs immigrés) in 1976 and then by the League for Human Rights in 1985. For all of them, the preconditions for giving local political rights were namely a constitutional reform allowing all foreign residents to vote in local elections. But, before the pressure of the European issue, such a project appeared as anti-constitutional and politically dangerous (this second argument has remained unchanged for extra-Europeans for whom a risk of foreign intrusion is evoked). Even if the constitutional reform of 1992[6] was not dictated by the mobilisation of the '*beurs*' for civic rights, the debate has been brought before by them and the idea that one could be a local citizen in a state in which he is not a national had begun to progress in minds. But the reform did not benefit to those who were claiming local rights, because only the Europeans, according to the principle of reciprocity, can now be citizens in a country where they are not nationals, although the effectiveness of this principle has not yet been implemented. Another juridical debate brought by immigration to European citizenship is convergence of nationality codes among European countries. It is one of the paradoxes of European citizenship: the game is the same for all citizens, based on reciprocal rights for nationals of all member countries of the European Union, but each country has the right to define by its own rule who is a European citizen and who is not. For the last ten years, immigration has much contributed to introducing debates on the reform of nationality rights, namely in France (1987-

[5] J. Leca, S. Bouamama. *et al.*, *La Citoyenneté dans tous ses états,* Paris, L'Harmattan, 1995.
[6] See D. Lochak: 'Les socialistes et l'immigration,' in O. Le Cour Grandmaison and C. Wihtol de Wenden, *Les Etrangers dans la cité,* expériences européennes, Paris, La Découverte, 1993, pp. 43-63, p. 55.

1993, 1997-1998) and in Germany (1999), claiming more convergence and focusing on the weight of colonial pasts: a debate for the future. Inversely, European citizenship cannot be opposed to extra-European countries.[7]

Cultural inputs Two main cultural inputs have been introduced by immigration in the content of European citizenship:

- citizenship conceived as membership: the long-term residents of extra-European countries are deprived of the freedom, of settlement and of work in Europe. This is the consecration of an evolution in the concept of citizenship: the Marshallian definition of citizenship as a membership seems to have gained on the French one, based on social contract and loyalty of allegiances. A more utilitarian use of citizenship prevails, as it is defined in the treaty of Maastricht not substantially changed in this regard in the Treaty of Amsterdam.[8] As the duties are low, European citizenship looks like a club with members who share the same aspirations and interests. Those who are members are supposed to have other values, external or transnational.
- multiculturalism: if ethnicity seems to be opposed to the building of a European culture which tries to define a non conflictual culture far from cultural ghettos,[9] multiculturalism seems to be an unavoidable dimension of European citizenship. The debates, successes and failures of it in some European countries, relate to immigration (namely in Germany and in the Netherlands in the late 1980s) have contributed to define which multiculturalism we should want for Europe: not fragmented identities, nor cultures with unequal status towards others (i.e. folklorized and despised), but a multiculturalism able to include Islam[10] and to consider that the unique definition of Europe is not Christianty, stressing on European cultural specificities beyond national stories: philosophy of the enlightenment's, liberalism, socialism, nationalism, industrial revolution, secularism, democracy.[11] In such a debate on addition or convergence of cultures, the story of integration has tought that there are different levels of identities: one is not less European if he feels French and the manner in which he is Catholic or Muslim is different from the manner in which he feels European or French. There is a multilaterality of choices and references and various forms of loyalism in Europe because European citizenship is not an addition of

[7] In the list of countries exempted from delivering visas by the United States (established on 1/5/1997) most European countries are included, except Portugal and Greece. See also : S. O'Leary and T. Tilikainen, *Citizenship and Nationality Status in the New Europe*, London, IPPR, Sweet and Maxwell, 1998, p.261.

[8] C. Wihtol de Wenden, *La Citoyenneté européenne, Paris, Presses de* Sciences Po, 1997, p.108.

[9] M. Martiniello, *Sortir des ghettos culturels*, Paris, Presses de Sciences Po, 1997.

[10] Another aspect of multiculturalism is the question introduced by the long-term presence of Muslims in Europe, a status for Islam in nation-states, which have not the same definition of secularism.

[11] Y. Salesse, *Propositions pour une Europe démocratique*, Paris, Ed. du Félin, 1997.

identities which mutually challenge themselves. This does not prevent Europe from having some contradictions in its recognition of minorities between the Council of Europe and the European Commission.

Civic values

Anti-racism the right to stay and move, family reunification: the third level brought by immigration to the content of European citizenship is the civic one. By its mobilization around anti-racism, right to stay and move, family reunification (three main claims put ahead by several civic associations such as the European Forum of Migrants in Brussels), it has introduced new civic values not formerly registered in the classical definition of 1789. These values are not only universal but they are particularly acute in the management of European policies of immigration and of 'living together'. There are also many values for a citizenship beyond the nation-state.

Multiple allegiances the right to multiple allegiances while being a national of a European country has been introduced by the debate around the reform of the nationality code in France, double citizenship in France and Germany, by the Gulf War and military service of Franco-Algerians and by the various 'veil' affairs: loyalty with multiple allegiances has been launched as a new trend, without inducing ethnic votes in most European countries, even if managing ethnicity with citizenship remains ambiguous.[12]

Limits

If immigration seems to have brought some positive debates in the context of European citizenship, the success remains limited.

A hierarchized citizenship with a new internal border The topic of citizenship of residence has been lost against that of citizenship of reciprocity. European citizenship is a series of concentric circles but with a main border between Europeans and extra-Europeans and a central issue, the freedom of circulation or not. This border is today reinforced by the dynamic of social inclusion/exclusion which partly corresponds with that of extra-European immigration, from which may appear an identity of dissent. As European identity has to be found on shared values and actual aspirations (and not as a static attribute) the risk of a gap between the firsts and the seconds may be opened between middle classes sharing a soft consensus on European citizenship and the others, relegated to identity consciousness.

A European citizenship against immigration and Islam Linked to the first one, another risk lies in the framing of the cultural content of cultural citizenship: as it is on search of itself, Europe may build its identity exclusively between

[12] V. Geisser, *Ethnicité républicaine*, Paris, Presses de Sciences Po, 1997, 261 p.

Europeans, their history, their culture in a tough definition of the supposed 'ancestors,' 'emblematic heroes' and more recent political leaders. As most of community feelings have been built in the past with 'the identification of a common enemy' (the nerve of nationalism and patriotism in Europe), the risk is that, lacking strong identity, Europeans may stress in symbolic imaginary border around Islam, illegal, those who are not 'de souche,' according to a rebuilt identity.

A European citizenship with the big market as its own value Another risk is the total failure of content for European citizenship: the only community would be that of free trade, with urbany practices for those who participate in it, sharing a common language. A civility could take birth from economy and welfare, featuring another border with those who have access or not to it (related by the debates around the access to education, medical care, social help for illegals). It is another definition of citizenship in western democracies which may gain some strength.

Conclusion

Immigration has played a part in the building of European citizenship. This citizenship, institutionally closed to Europeans is not yet culturally closed because its content has to be framed. Its borders are less territorial than symbolic, defining other spaces than those built by Mediterranean history, Europe of Renaissance, Great Empires and 'Concert of Nations'. Its cultural community may be defined by the story and the space of people living there ('l'espace des gens') and the consciousness people have to live this space inside the European framework. So, citizenship of residence, multiculturalism, participation, plurality of references and choices could have some role in European citizenship in search of its sense.

Chapter 6

Change and Continuity in French Islam

Rémy Leveau

Introduction

Painting a picture of Islam in France at the start of the 21st Century by looking at the last decade involves highlighting perceptions and stereotypes that increasingly determine community-based attitudes. First, though, we have to explain how this religion, seen as foreign and aggressive (to go by the symbols of the Battle of Poitiers, the Crusades and other events), became in the 1980s the second biggest religion in France, and of the French.

It happened without any invasion or large-scale conversions but simply through *jus soli* (the law of the soil) after Muslim immigrants from North Africa had arrived in France. The same thing occurred in other Northern European countries from 1974 on, when these countries stopped immigration and said they were discreetly turning people back.

North Africans in France, Turks in Germany and Indians and Pakistanis in Britain all flocked to take part in the industrial rebuilding and expansion after World War II. Most came as single people and were mainly seen as simple workers who had left Islam back home with their families. But when the governments of both host countries and native countries agreed to encourage them to go home in return for economical aid from Europe, this clashed with their personal and family ambitions. What happened was an assertion of identity that became a social movement with the state as main intermediary.

This rise of a group of people who became visible and organised in response to the ideas others had about them shook up the political agreements that, at the end of the 19th Century or even earlier, had governed relations between religion and politics after conflicts mainly involving Christian churches.

The crisis in 1989 over whether some Muslim girls should be allowed to wear traditional headscarfs to school was a symbolical turning-point. The government immediately protested against this Muslim demand and French society at large rejected it. But during the 1990-1991 Gulf War, the government used its connections with the Muslim community to ensure order in city suburbs with strong immigrant populations.

In 1995 however, terrorist incidents aimed at getting suburban youth to revolt against the government revived the old images of a Muslim community supposedly introducing controversial issues from outside French society. But the dramatic violence did not affect the desire by most Muslims to be absorbed into that society. The growing affirmation of a Muslim identity in Europe that would have real decision-making power is ultimately a big threat to efforts by the Muslim community to increasingly assert themselves as partners of the French state.

The new drive for religious identity also indirectly affects relations between Europe and the immigrants' home countries because the latter try to keep control of their departed citizens through religion. They also fear emergence in Europe of an urban, modern Islamic vanguard whose pluralist approach would compete with the conservative and controlled version of Islam back home. This is a new issue in relations between Europe and its Mediterranean neighbours.

These are the main things that have shaken up relations between politics and religion over the past nearly 30 years.

Building an Islam that affirms the identity of immigrants who arrived in the 1970s

North African immigrants in France were seen at first as part of 'capitalism's reserve army,' recruited to build up competition that would force down the wages of the host society's existing working class, or were regarded as people from recently decolonised Third World countries. But they gradually asserted themselves as Muslims through untypical and uncoordinated protests in declining industries, housing situations and symbolical places such as schools. These conflicts arose from the absence or collapse of old-fashioned handling of social relationships and led to new ways of integrating that stressed the group rather than the individual. No clear rules were established and new forms of social organization were simply superimposed on the old in a haphazard and sometimes conflicting way.

Industrial disputes involving skilled workers in the motor industry, where Islam took root in the 1970s, were about changing working conditions and the switch from the Ford assembly-line system to automation. This transition involved laying off almost the entire old immigrant workforce that had got used to the Ford system, as had the peasants and southern European immigrants before them.

When the changeover came, nobody defended their interests properly – neither the political parties (mostly the communists) nor the trade unions (mainly the Communist-linked CGT) that had played a leading part in integrating the previous generation of workers. The parties and unions had other things to do than take up the cause of groups, rather than individuals, who did not at the time seem to be future voters or long-term supporters. The request to defend their interests clashed with the push to get new jobs and social security benefits for the earlier generation of immigrants who were mostly well-represented in the parties and unions. The strikes and hard-line communist attitudes of the post-World War II period had managed to integrate into society the old generation of immigrants but could no longer be used in the same way.

Compared with these examples of successful and mainly individual integration of Italian and Polish workers, the North Africans seemed an untypical and temporary element. They came from countries that had only just emerged from sometimes long and violent colonial wars of independence, so did not seek French citizenship and the government hardly thought of suggesting it to them.

But they refused to be victims or rejects of a technological transition they had been involved in as labourers. They demanded the right to stay and freely plan their future, setting themselves apart from the French or North African governments that tried to tell them what they should do. This put them in conflict with both the previous generation of immigrant workers defended by the political parties and the unions and with the North African governments that seemed ready to negotiate their forcible return home in exchange for wholesale economical aid for their resettlement there which they would manage themselves.

In their isolation, the new immigrants instinctively turned to Islam as the only legitimate way they could both assert themselves as a group and defend their individual interests before the employers, in competition with other workers in crisis and with the threat of their native countries abandoning them for financial aid from the rich countries.

Their assertion of identity included requests for prayer rooms in the workplace and adjustment of working hours to allow them to worship. Starting out with spontaneous requests from small groups, Muslims in the same workplace eventually began acting together to negotiate with employers and unions about respecting religious practices, which they said was a matter of human rights.

These groups meant the management lost some control over running the shop-floor and arranging working hours to 'imams,' either self-styled or accepted by the Muslim group. These workplace imams quickly became negotiators with management and unions, as intermediaries or mediators in disputes. They were not able to stop factory closures or automation, but they did enable orderly solutions that looked after workers' interests and respected their dignity.

This made the harshest periods of layoffs less violent affairs than they had been earlier when the workers were unorganised, ill-informed, traumatised by change and liable to take hard-line stands. The effect of taking account of a demand connected with religious identity was to recreate a form of communication, resolve various problems and help people accept an inevitable development.

A similar change was seen in places where immigrants lived and strikes broke out in worker hostels in the 1970s. The handling of rent disputes led to establishment of an accepted religious authority in hostels where most residents were Muslims. Other effects of a community structure were that rules accepted by the group, such as a ban on alcohol and observance of Ramadan,[1] could be imposed on those culturally considered Muslims. The replacement of bars in the hostels by prayer rooms and the emergence of imams led to more orderly settlement of disputes that used to take a more radical turn.

[1] The month of the Islamic calendar (the Hegira) during which Muslims fast for part of each day as a demonstration of piety.

The achievements of the Mitterrand period

The religious presence grew, usually little noticed, from 1981 (the year François Mitterrand became president) when foreigners were given the right to set up voluntary association by simply declaring their existence. The proliferation of such cultural associations met the need for facilities to practice Islam because it meant a lot more places of prayer, which were called mosques though they were not traditional buildings that looked like the mosques in Muslim countries. Every time there was a move for greater visibility, local authorities resisted through use of urban planning rules and the government did nothing to prevent this. However when the Muslims did win permission to build a large mosque at the new town of Évry, near Paris, the government accepted or encouraged requests to help building a cathedral so the mosque would not be the town's most visible public building.

These achievements, which helped create a legal framework for collective action, were accompanied by measures benefiting individuals, including 10-year residence cards and the steady granting of French nationality to educated Muslims. Affirming one's Islamic identity became commonplace without losing any of its vitality.

The collective images and perceptions of Islam this generates help create a profile of the group and help to understand what is increasingly seen as a community approach. But in surveys, some people considered culturally Muslim refuse to recognise themselves as such. Others say religion is a private matter and stress their professional or national identity. The deliberate omission of questions about religion on census forms and in most public opinion surveys means researchers and officials do not have concrete data to go on.

Most of the time, they make estimates based on the original nationality of immigrants or their parents that are harder and harder to use because under the French system, nationality is acquired through being born in France *(jus soli)*. Taking all this into account, the number of Muslims in France is put at between three passed half and five million, which easily makes Islam the second biggest religion in France and among French citizens.

The vast majority (over two million) of these 'sociological' Muslims are from North Africa, more than half of them from Algeria and most of them French nationals. To this total must be added the Harkis (Algerians who fought on the French side during the independence war and their descendants). Getting French nationality is easier for Algerians living in France because Algeria was French until 1962 and a child of Algerian parents born in France since then is automatically French. After the Algerians come the Moroccans (800,000), who are now the biggest group acquiring French nationality, and Tunisians (500,000). There are also half a million Turks and about half a million Muslims from West Africa and the Indian Oceans islands of Réunion and the Comoros.

Each group remains marked by its history and its homeland and they gather at the places of prayer according to these differences. The religious language is usually Arabic or Turkish but sometimes sermons *(khotba)* are delivered in French. The experience of Strasbourg shows how very hard it is to get different groups of Muslims in the same place of prayer. French nationality opens up many areas of the national and local civil service (police, hospitals, railways and the army) to groups that have often been discriminated against in the labour market for ethnical reasons, have stayed in low-level jobs and are plagued with very high unemployment (over 20 per cent) among young people, including graduates.

Since 1998, the government has unofficially exercised positive discrimination towards these groups in state-funded youth employment schemes in the hope of eventually absorbing them into the labour force through the civil service. These efforts help offset the racism and discrimination they face in looking for work. Such workers are however slowly penetrating the services sector, where large firms have a more liberal attitude than medium-sized companies.

France does not have as many ethnical firms as neighbouring countries do. A community-oriented social economy – getting jobs for graduates and supplementing the work of local officials – is to be found more among associations, which receive state or local government funding. This still partial opening-up should grow as representatives of these ethnical groups enter political life, where Muslim immigrants are the biggest pool of voters.

Several hundred local elected officials, a few members of the European Parliament (elected under proportional representation) are the vanguard of this. The current voting system for deputies and senators is not very favourable to ethnical candidates. But during the 2002 presidential and parliamentary elections, iconic figures such as the captain of the French football team, Zinédine Zidane, will be much sought after to endorse various candidates. The 'beur' vote usually goes to the left-wing parties, but the right and even the extreme-right are making an effort to woo voters at local level.

So Muslim immigrants will probably behave the same way as the earlier generation of immigrants, trading their votes for social assistance and job creation, especially at local level. Assimilation therefore works and interaction is more group than individual through use of community associations and social assistance policies. Since 1981, these policies have taken care to create conditions for integration without violence, refusing to respond officially to the demands of a group or community but unofficially doing so case by case, leaving aside the principle of everyone being equal in the government's eyes.

Paradoxically, the achievements of the Mitterrand period included playing down the nationality of an immigrant or a French citizen. French nationality is often seen, in the words of A. Sayad, as a 'vaccination against expulsion.' Religious affiliation is now the important thing and is seen as a primary loyalty to a national group. If you are officially French, it is easier to affirm Muslim identity on grounds of basic human rights.

Challenging the secular accord and the civic model

This attitude came to make Islam seem like an obstacle in negotiations over the main aspects of a new kind of social change not well understood by French society. But firms and housing officials, for example, did not resist Islam as much as the government or local officials.

The presence of the so-called Islamic veil, or headscarf, in state schools from 1989 led to a widely-publicised major dispute. Wearing it to school is considered harmless in most European countries but it set off a row in France because it was seen as a act of religious aggression in a public place and contrary to the 1905 official separation of church and state. The rules and legal precedents banning Christian crosses in state schools were immediately cited. The schoolgirls wearing the scarves at first had no intention of challenging authority. But associations quickly took a stand defending and supporting them and even went as far as accusing the government and forcing it to change its attitude to fall in line with European Union rules on such matters.

The conflict then did an about-turn, with the majority reacting as if they were a threatened minority. The situation was complicated by the provocative image of Islam created by events in Iran and later Algeria and the headscarf was seen as a symbol of *jihad*, or holy war. The high fertility rates in Islamic countries were unfairly associated with North African immigrants and depicted as a kind of weapon that would turn French society into a multicultural one like Britain or the United States. Other bogies were used to stir up people's anxiety about social change and turn them against a socialist government accused by the right and the far right of wanting to encourage Muslim immigration.

When the government of Prime Minister Pierre Mauroy gave foreigners the right to form their own associations, this unintentionally included religious ones. Introduction of a 10-years residence card ended the worries of immigrants about whether they could legally stay in France. This moved closer to virtually granting French nationality to immigrant children born in France. A kind of halfway-house developed, without the state formally recognising Islam as an entity to be negotiated with as in Belgium.

In the French system, developed during the 19th Century after the turmoil of the Revolution, the state chooses those it wants to represent a community. It gives them recognition and funding so they can build up a constituency and play their full part as intermediaries. This is how the state, while giving a leading role to the Catholic Church until 1905, was able to incorporate Protestants and Jews as recognised minorities and create conditions in which they could worship and maintain their group identity through such things as places of worship, cemeteries, ritual slaughterhouses, schools and hospitals.

The state wants to offer the same set-up to the Muslims, but they mostly fail to grasp the issues involved in building a pluralistic system that consigns religion to a person's private life. They are prepared to drop many attitudes inherited from being part of a Muslim majority in their home country, but do not see the need to fully join a secular accord made before they came along and in conditions that do not entirely suit them.

As the most recent arrivals on the religious scene, the Muslims have inherited no places of worship provided by the state, as the Protestants did after the 1801 Concordat. Neither can they look to a prosperous community to fund their development. The recourse to their home countries or to rich Arab states such as Saudi Arabia makes them dependent, which are later reproached for. One solution may be to officially recognise a religious authority in charge of food laws (*halal* meat) and funded by the faithful.

The problem has been around since the early 1980s. Every time a government agency wanted to designate religious officials to do this and collect taxes, the Muslim community protested, along with Islamic officials abroad who felt excluded. Institutionalising Islam by directives from the top satisfied nobody and could not last, whether done by left-wing interior Ministers such as Pierre Joxe and Jean-Pierre Chevènement, or those on the right such as Charles Pasqua. The policy was based on the inability of the Muslim community to appoint representatives acceptable to the government. The various religious groups claiming to speak for the community were not keen to agree to anything unless it gave them dominance in the community. The government deplored the confusion and fragmentation but in fact adapted to it. A strong and firmly-based Muslim religious leadership would have been more worrying.

The government says religious representatives are needed, but in fact it wants to give priority to civic groups, providing Muslims with some voice without too much religious content. Associations such as France Plus, SOS Racisme, directed from above, have emerged to play this role without referring to Islam but still gathering Muslims together and putting them in a milieu going well beyond Islam. So the civic message takes precedence over religion, which finds its place in the multitude of local cultural associations that serve at least partly as religious organizations. All this provides intermediaries, as well as building an infrastructure and creating a degree of representation, with everyone content to keep up the ambiguity.

Political parties, trade unions and town authorities look to the associations for potential voters or supporters. The association leaders play along and find opportunities to move up in the society that the usual channels do not provide. This meeting of conflicting but reconcilable interests has hitherto met basic needs. It is not the cultural and religious recognition of Islam wanted by the parties involved, but it has compensated for various failings of government policy and the way the whole system works.

First of all, it is a short cut to putting Islam on an equal footing with other religions. The cautious attitude suited governments of right and left, who were both afraid the far right would exploit the issue.

The prolific growth of community associations also partly made up for the political and economical failure to assimilate immigrants. Having a vote and a chance to become a citizen did not really produce a national Muslim leadership, but handing over administration to the associations in the 1990s created a temporary elite with limited powers looking after a local community or a particular field.

This can also be seen as economical compensation, with the associations functioning as a sort of ethnical business operation, receiving a lot of public money in the form of subsidies. In Germany, economical integration of immigrants is much more important, through creation of links between Turkish immigrants and the host society, alongside more limited political integration and less activity by associations than in France.

Islam in France was also affected in the 1990s by tensions arising from the community's real or supposed links with the outside world. During the 1990-91 Gulf War, France joined an international coalition opposing Iraqi ruler Saddam Hussein, whose appeal for a *jihad* provoked huge anti-Western street demonstrations in Algiers and Tunis. But the French city suburbs stayed calm and surveys among French Muslims showed their steady loyalty to the French state and its leader. The government appealed directly to the Muslim community not to import external conflicts into the French situation.

They were not so successful in 1995-96 when extremist violence linked to the Algerian civil war led to plane hijackings and bomb attacks in France. The incidents were spectacular but had only a small impact on the community and the extremists were rejected by young people in the suburbs who chose not to endanger their integration into French society. Efforts to build a community involved a continuation of a difficult dialogue with the state rather than resorting to violence. The clashes in Jerusalem in Autumn 2000 brought the Palestinian *intifada* to the city suburbs and anti-Jewish demonstrations occurred. But again, Islamic community leaders reaffirmed their loyalty to the state and their opposition to importing violent quarrels from the outside.

A growing European dimension

The problem of institutionalising Islam as an identity connected to immigrants from Africa who settle in declining industrial areas is now a Europe-wide phenomenon. The free movement within the continent of its legal residents encourages assimilation and negotiation for advantages obtained in different countries, more in terms of human rights than religion.

Europe introduces a new dimension, as a kind of appeal mechanism in a very lopsided dialogue between governments and individuals. It is not totally opposed to the idea of a community and protecting minority rights but rather than being a focus of identification is more an authority that harmonises and mediates and extends its influence to the countries of origin.

The Barcelona Process that followed the Oslo/Washington Middle East accords involves all the Mediterranean countries where the vast majority of Muslims in Europe come from and includes security, cultural and economical aspects. Its implementation will create a basis for dialogue and solidarity with the immigrants' home countries, avoid provocative labels and look after the external side of an integration process influenced by real or imagined links with Palestinians or with Bosnia, as well as tensions in North Africa.

It involves identifying with a future European Islam through its local chapters, from Marseilles to Hamburg, and with an external Islam, a kind of externalised painful memory of the trauma of one's personal exile. Through this filter, a range of compromises is being made, much bigger ones than observers generally note. Identification with painful memories of what happened elsewhere do not lead to violence or diminish loyalty. This was evident during external crises such as the Gulf War, the Algerian civil war and the violence in Jerusalem. French

Muslims stress their allegiance to the state by focusing on the person of the President (François Mitterrand or Jacques Chirac) and have no intention of endangering their right to peaceful residence in France.

At a deeper level, the line about external solidarity hides the practice of mingling different societies, disregarding bans on inter-marriage, mixing with other cultures at school and in the workplace. Nationality stops being a problem as soon as members of the host society recognise a person's right to have a different background.

The trend towards Europeanising Islam is still for the moment being done more by comparison than regulation. This does not rule out future transnational intervention in the field of religious standards and values despite religion not being part of the European Union's mandate. Immigration, right of asylum and the status of minorities are ways of getting round this. Reworking pluralist compromises between religion and politics can only be done at this level, by including Islam as a legitimate component of European culture and identity.

This assumes Europe will come up with a non-antagonistic view of Islam and can create neighbourly aid-based relationships with the southern and eastern Mediterranean Muslim countries most of the immigrants come from. It also assumes that Muslims in Europe undertake a theological review of the practice of Islam as a minority religion in a Christian-based urban society and sort out practical problems of coexisting with other religions.

Today it is less a matter of settling details of disputes about conversion or mixed marriages than about the status of women and the relationship with those who have left the Muslim community. This can be rather tricky because solutions arrived at in a European Islamic context may also influence countries with Islamic majorities and trigger developments the rulers of these countries would like to delay as long as possible.

The relationship with the home countries is complicated too because Islam may seem a way to stay loyal to the community in return for using and having less respect for being a national of either France or the countries of North Africa. Muslim immigrants are not all zealous opponents of their home governments like the Cubans in Miami. But neither do they echo their policies. They are cautious because they want to protect family members left behind from reprisals, retain their right to visits to their native country and keep two passports, but they also have an assertive approach and bring images of life in Europe to the southern Mediterranean.

The interests of the home countries and their diasporas ultimately diverge but each tries to gloss over any conflict. The long-term danger is probably from mixed marriages (half of all Algerian immigrants make them) and from a kind of group identity loss that waters down the observance of Islam as it does for other religions in the big cities (Paris, Lyon, Marseilles) and northeastern France, where most French Muslims live today.

Chapter 7

Citizenship: Beyond Blood and Soil*

Riva Kastoryano

Introduction

Citizenship has become a major topic of discussion in politics and social science since the 1980s. It involves both law and political philosophy and lies at the heart of Europe's debate about the rights of immigrant workers in host countries and, more broadly, the building of the continent itself. These two apparently independent issues raise questions about the relevance of today's nation-state and the citizenship-nationality link it.

Citizenship and nationality – two interdependent and 'interchangeable'[1] notions that are part of the nation-state – can best be defined as a person's membership of a political community. This becomes real through rights (social, political and cultural) and duties that are the essence of citizenship. The legal step that officializes it implies incorporation of the 'foreigner' into the national community, whose moral and political values he is expected to share. He is also expected to adopt the community's historical points of reference and make them his own as proof of full adherence and loyalty to the founding tenets of the nation which, according to Eugen Weber, is the only sense of community that modern times have produced.

Debate about citizenship revolves round these expectations and is thus linked to debate about the nation-state – its formation, its political traditions and national identity. France and Germany have contrasting approaches to citizenship and nationality because of their different histories and political traditions. France, the model nation-state, sees itself as universalist by virtue of being assimilationist and egalitarian. Its elective and political concept of a nation contrasts with Germany's cultural and ethnical notion of it based on having common ancestors and belonging to the same cultural community. This is expressed through different ways of granting citizenship – in France largely based on 'the law of the soil' and in Germany exclusively according to 'the law of blood.'[2]

* Parts of this article are published in U. Hedetoft and M. Hjort (eds.), *The Postnational Self*, Minnesota University Press, 2002, forth coming.

[1] J. Leca, 'Nationalité et citoyenneté dans l'Europe des immigrations,' J. Costa-Lascoux and P. Weil, *Logiques d'État et immigration en Europe*, Kimé, Paris 1992.

[2] *Cf.* W. R. Brubaker, *Citizenship and Nationhood in France and Germany*, Harvard University Press, Cambridge, MA 1992. L. Dumont, *L'Idéologie allemande. France-Allemagne et retour*, eds. Gallimard, Paris 1991.

But things are more complex than this. How a nation sees itself, its idea of citizenship and how that links to nationality obviously affects the goals of immigrant activists and how they participate in the host society. But civic action that expresses an immigrant's political involvement goes beyond a simple legal definition because it works in different fields and in different ways. It also operates just as much inside a cultural, ethnical, religious or what Jean Leca[3] calls a 'temporary' community as it does in a national one. The resulting multiple identities exist alongside a republican vision of citizenship that not only recognises just the individual but also raises the issue of the loyalty of individuals and groups to the nation. Such multiple allegiances, though common in all plural societies, mean that the French and German states have a suspicious attitude to immigrants, which rears its head in any debate about immigration and citizenship.

So the issue of citizenship opens the way to negotiations about identity between states and immigrants.[4] States have to negotiate new ways and means of incorporating immigrants and their children into the political community based on a different balance between new community structures and national institutions. Relying on the principle of equality, individuals and groups have to fight against any kind of political, social or cultural exclusion. From this comes a demand for recognition as a 'liberal, republican citizen'[5]loyal to both the nation and to a community and identity that is not a national one. This automatically challenges the traditional link between the cultural community and political belonging – the first as a source of identity and the second as a right to civic participation with equal rights.

This development is strengthened by the process of building a single Europe, which proliferates allegiances of both individuals and groups and makes more fuzzy the divide between citizenship and nationality, law and identity and politics and culture. This article attempts to show how these different views of citizenship relate to each other through the political action that nourishes them. Also how, despite activity taking place in a transnational arena, the demand for recognition that guides the strategies of the players involved remains within the bounds of the legitimacy of the state, and how despite the different areas in which citizenship is expressed (associations, cultural and ethnical communities and civil society), only 'legal' citizenship allows individuals and groups to take part in the political community in the broad sense.

[3] J. Leca, 'Après Maastricht sur la prétendue résurgence du nationalisme,' *in Témoin*, n°1, pp. 29-38.

[4] R. Kastoryano, *La France, l'Allemagne et leurs immigrés. Négocier l'identité,* Armand Colin, Paris 1997.

[5] *Cf.* R. Dagger, *Civic Virtues, Rights, Citizenship and Republican Liberalism,* Oxford University Press, New York 1997.

The status of citizen

France's system, combining the law of the soil (*jus soli*) and the law of blood (*jus sanguinis*), and the German one that is still based on descendance from common ancestors exclusively by the law of blood, sum up the different approaches of the two nation-states, their creation and construction, their values and their founding tenets, in short, their ideology. They are also at the root of any vision of the nation or state to be passed on to future generations and 'newcomers.'

In France, what the law says about nationality aims to keep to the republican tradition, 'incorporating foreigners' children born in France into the civic community ... in the name of equality and universalism.'[6] This can be described as 'French-style integration,' which is the title of a 1993 report by the High Commission for Integration. The notion refers to French-ness and its importance in assimilating foreigners. The report says it is 'the deep-rooted purpose of our country which, inspired by the principles of the Declaration of the Rights of Man, proclaims the equality of all through the diversity of their cultures.'

The principle is based on the idea of the nation as an elective entity, the product of 'a daily plebiscite,' to borrow the slogan Renan used in a lecture at the Sorbonne on 11 March 1882 called 'What is a nation?.' In this way, the French nation, as an 'ideal nation,' feeds the republican ideology and vice-versa, and it is up to the state's institutions to maintain and perpetuate this political tradition and ensure the wholeness of the nation by training 'republican citizens' whose only so-called public identity is belonging to the nation. This is what turns 'the peasant,'[7] the foreigner or the immigrant into a French person, making the France a collection of regional, cultural and even religious differences from which to build a nation. Today, France describes itself retrospectively as 'a country of immigration.'[8]

Germany, however, says it is not a country of immigration. The official line to this effect is based on the concept of a nation as one stressing the rights of blood and organic links between people having the same language, culture and most of all the same ancestors. In France, citizenship is inclusive, in Germany it is exclusive. France is a nation that sees itself as universalist, while Germany is one that wants to be exclusive, based on a feeling of belonging to a culture and a people. This feeling came from the German Romantic movement that emerged in the early 19th Century and grew in reaction to the rationalism that inspired the French Revolution and its universal values. Cultural unity (*Fichte*) and unity of language (preached by Herder) fed the German dream of national unity and limited collective identity to those who had the same ancestors, the same language and the same culture. The notion of *Volksgeist* (spirit of a people), which shows how far Germany is from the ideas of the Enlightenment, became the basis of the German

[6] R. Brubaker, *op. cit.* 1992. G. Noiriel, *op. cit.* 1987 (quoted by the Weil report, La documentation Française, Paris 1997).

[7] A reference to the English title of a book by E. Weber called *From Peasant into Frenchman.*

[8] *Cf.* G. Noiriel, *Le Creuset français,* Seuil, Paris 1988. M. Tribalat, *Cent ans d'immigration en France,* PUF, Paris, and M. Tribalat, *Faire France,* La Découverte, Paris 1996.

nation.[9] The concept of *Volksnation* (nation of a people), as opposed to the French ideal of a *Staats(burger)nation,* also developed.

These approaches show up clearly when ideas meet the law, when principles confront reality. Despite changes over time in the criteria for obtaining nationality and changes in the laws of both countries, these principles underpin declarations and discussion, pointing to a historical continuity as if to maintain their national differences.

In France, naturalization is always seen as a way to assimilate foreigners. But economic and demographic necessity waters these principles down. In 1804, the principle that every child born on French soil is French (*jus soli*) was rejected by a court and descendance was introduced as a criteria for getting nationality, meaning that a child born of a French parent was French. Since then, a combination of *jus soli* and *jus sanguinis* has developed case by case.

In the 19th Century, military concerns produced measures to force the grandchildren of immigrants (the double *jus soli* law of 1851) and then the children of immigrants (*jus soli* in 1889) to serve in the French armed forces. After World War I, those who had been killed had to be replaced and naturalization of foreigners was made easier (law of 10 August 1927). Foreigners were seven per cent of the population in 1918. The ministerial directive of 13 August 1927 said that 'while the law had previously implied that legal assimilation of immigrants took precedence over de facto assimilation, now the two will proceed in parallel.'[10] Today the right to nationality combines *jus sanguinis* and *jus soli,* as well as a desire to be naturalised. This right dates from a 1945 statute concerning the Nationality Law, making the right no longer part of Common Law.

Naturalization changes as government policy on integration of foreigners changes. Marriage or period of residence, 'good moral character' and knowledge of the French language and culture from living in the society remain the chief requirements for admission to the political community. In 1987, the Advisory Commission on Nationality said young foreigners born in France also had to express a wish to become French, meaning they had to apply for it instead of it being automatic. This took effect in 1993. The most recent law, passed by parliament in 1997, abolished the 'wish' requirement and restored that of simple proof of birth on French soil. When the law was voted on and minister Elisabeth Guigou said France had assimilated such people in practice and would now assimilate them by law, she was just voicing her attachment to France's political traditions. The number of people who acquired nationality doubled between 1973 and 1993 (from 33,616 to 73,164). 'Declarations of nationality' and naturalizations grew by 3.5 per cent in 1985 and by 1.8 per cent in 1989 and continued to increase by an average 2.2 per cent a year.[11]

[9] R. Brubaker, *op. cit.*, p. 9.

[10] *Être français aujourd'hui et demain,* vol. 2, p. 27.

[11] A. Lebon, *Regards sur l'immigration et la présence étrangère en France,* La documentation Française, Paris 1990, p. 23. *Situation de l'immigration et de la présence étrangère en France, 1993-94,* La documentation Française, Paris 1994, pp. 32-34.

In Germany, the term 'importing workers' is used, rather than immigration. Even the switch from being a country of emigration to being one of immigration, changing the statistics, has not brought any changes in the law. The presence of foreigners has not altered the laws about 'German-ness' and German nationality which, although challenged as being anti-democratic, seem consistent with how they define the German nation.

That nation is defined as a shared culture and the basic qualification for nationality is still having similar ancestors through the law of blood. The concept of *Das deutsche Volk* (the German people) offers such a version of belonging, ruling out any cultural differences by making cultural unity and the organic nature of the national community part of the definition of the nation. But nationality based on the law of blood posed a conceptual and practical problem when the unified German state was founded in 1871 because the new frontiers of the empire brought into contact different ideas about what a people and a territory were.

Little Germany excluded from the nation foreigners from neighbouring countries and automatically included ethnic Germans who lived beyond its borders. Rogers Brubaker notes that this produced two kinds of citizenship – one political, based on territory, and the other spiritual and ethnic, based on common ancestors.[12] So German nationality combined ancestors and territory (the past) so Germans outside the borders of the state would at least retain German nationality. German-ness (*Deutschtum*) also theoretically included Germans living in neighbouring countries because they qualified as belonging to the German people as defined. A 1913 law about 'belonging to the state and the Empire' strengthened the ethnic aspect of citizenship by allowing Germans living outside Germany to keep their German nationality but ruling out giving German nationality to foreigners born on German soil.

In 1949, the Basic Law of the Federal German Republic confirmed the notion of citizenship founded on belonging to the German people. In its article 116, it says a German is anyone of German descent living within the borders of the Empire. This justified giving citizenship to people returning to Germany after the collapse of the Soviet bloc who could prove their German ancestry (the *Aussiedler*). About 30,000 people benefited from this in 1988 and more than 100,000 in 1991. Their 'immigration' to Germany has been seen since 1989 as taking in political refugees.

Today, varying ideas of citizenship seem to be one of the results of the 1989 collapse of the Soviet bloc and the Berlin Wall. In 1990, a new law on foreigners (*Aussländergesetz*) was drawn up to make integration easier in reaction to the flow of people from the east. The law for the first time made socialization a requirement for grandchildren of *Gastarbeiter* seeking naturalization. It said young foreigners could obtain legal naturalization if they applied for it between the age of 16 and 23, had lived lawfully in Germany for the previous eight years, had attended school for the past six years (four of them in a non-specialist school) and had no police record. The cost of getting naturalised, until then between 3,000 and 5,000 DM, was reduced by 100 DM for these youngsters. But dual nationality was

[12] R. Brubaker, *op. cit.*

still not allowed. The number of foreigners naturalised, which grew between 20,000 and 30,000 each year from 1973 and 1989, reached 101,377 in 1990. In 1995, under the new coalition government, dual nationality was put back on the agenda.

After the racist attacks in Mölln and Solingen in the winter of 1992-1993, citizenship became more than ever a focus of debate, especially as the *Aussiedler* were given automatic citizenship, even though they are still seen today by politicians and the public as more 'foreign' than the 'blood foreigners'. They are even suspected of being behind the hatred of foreigners (*Ausländerfeindlichkeit*) that has increased since their arrival, and thus the cause of social unrest that has shaken official policy towards foreigners, forcing them to campaign for legal recognition of their presence in the form of citizenship.

In 1994, the new coalition government announced a measure affecting grand-children of Turkish immigrant families. Groups working with immigrants referred to the debate as being about 'child citizenship' (*Kindersstaatsangehörigkeit*). The aim of the draft law was first to give German citizenship to children born in Germany of foreign parents, from the time of birth if one of the parents was also born there or has been living here for the last eight years. This in effect introduced a 'double law of the soil,' already long recognised in France, but the married parents had to prove they had lived in Germany for at least 10 years before the child's birth. Also, when the child reached 18, it could reverse things by choosing between German nationality or that of its parents.

Recently, it has been proposed to grant such children a 'naturalization guarantee' (*Einbürgerungszusicherung*) that would be clearly marked on their birth certificate.[13] Though expressing a wish to be naturalised was offered, as in the French law of 1993, only one nationality could be chosen since dual nationality was not allowed. The battle for citizenship today centres on negotiations to permit dual nationality.

In both France and Germany, the extent of the debate clearly shows the fear of politicians and the public that nationality would be 'desecrated' for the sake of 'citizenship to get papers'. The arguments were based on the real or imagined attachment of the 'immigrants' or 'foreigners' to their nation-state of origin in the form of identification with an immigrant cultural community and an associated demand for a national or religious communal identity. In this sense, immigration is a challenge to the overall nature of citizenship and its inseparable link to nationality.

But the real challenge to national-states is the limitations of their laws and their relevance to society. Legal citizenship is not enough to cope with the problems of social exclusion in France and social and political exclusion in Germany. Battles for the right to equality as a citizen extend to different areas and the negotiations between vested interests become a kind of 'negotiation of identity' between the authorities and the immigrant population.[14]

[13] *La Lettre de la Citoyenneté*, n°31, Jan.-Feb. 1998.

[14] R. Kastoryano, *op. cit.*

The identity of citizen

In real life, citizenship is not confined to its legal definition, even if that is the most important thing in the political domain. In the 19th Century, the exercise of citizenship led to its extension to other areas such as health, education and access to social advantages in general. After World War II, as the result of a lecture given by a British sociologist T.H. Marshall, citizenship was reconsidered in terms of social class and became less a strictly legal and political concept and more a social one of equality before the law.[15]

As a general social right, citizenship is part of the fabric of political rights. But for foreign workers and their families, in both France and Germany, access to these rights is through the simple extension of social rights. This is because as soon as they arrived in the country they became 'social citizens' through their access to the same social advantages and the same constitutional protection of human rights as the natives. This is what Habermas calls 'passive citizenship' and its legitimacy is in the growth of the welfare state. The passage from this social citizenship to legal or 'active'[16] citizenship is made in their case through 'naturalization,' which takes into account the length of residence and the contribution to the society in the form of work and service, plus a 'natural' affinity.

But citizenship in practice means direct or indirect participation in public affairs by individuals as well as groups and immigrants as well as the rest of the population. It expresses an individual's commitment to the political community[17] and applies as much to officially-recognised associations and the activities of local cultural or ethnic communities – in fact civil society as a whole – as it does to the political community.

The differences between French and German citizenship laws are reflected in the kind of participation seen in each country and in the attitude of those who participate. But in both countries, the process of 'politicising identity' has led the 'immigrants' – legal citizens as some are in France or foreigners as in Germany – to take action in the political arena, a shared place of socialization and exercising power, to show their commitment and at least unofficial membership of the political community. Immigrants in both countries make such a commitment through associations that influence participation and launch the exercise of citizenship itself by creating a 'citizen identity' that develops in the course of activities.

Since the 1980s in both France and Germany, immigrant associations, backed by the authorities as long as their activities further the state's policy of

[15] T. H. Marshall, *Class, Citizenship and Social Development*, University of Chicago Press, Chicago 1964.

[16] The term used by J. Habermas *in* 'Citizenship and National Identity: Some Reflections on the Future of Europe' *in* R. Beiner (ed.) *Theorizing Citizenship*, State University of New York Press, Albany (NY) 1995, pp. 255-283.

[17] For citizenship as a feeling of belonging and citizenship as a commitment, see J. Leca 'Individualisme et citoyenneté,' *in* P. Birnbaum and J. Leca (eds.) *Sur l'individualisme*, Presses de la FNSP, Paris 1986, pp. 159-213.

integration, have become the means of political socialization for immigrant groups. In these associations, which are solidarity networks between people of the same national, regional, ethnic or religious origin, an identity aims to be collective. Limits are established, new solidarity fostered and the political rules of the game and how to cope with the state are learned. Discourse alternates with action and these community-based organizations appear more and more as a refuge, sometimes even a sanctuary, where a culture, a religion, an ethnicity and a nation take shape and take root in relation to the state to negotiate the status of each of these elements with the authorities.

This politicization of identity finds legitimacy in awareness of identity largely fed by public debate and boosted by local and national policies and targeted government action. But simple awareness of cultural differences very quickly turns into political action when accompanied by demands for recognition of these differences by the state. So their creation aims to foster both a collective awareness and incorporation into the structure of the state.

In other words, these associations inject identity interests – an 'us' – into political action and demands. Political participation is thus an extension of community mobilization and 'citizen identity' is rooted in the fight for universal values – the fight against racism and exclusion and in favour of equality. These values, the cement of the reconstituted cultural community, are also the values that bring immigrants into the national community. In the late 1980s, notably at the 1989 municipal elections, militants in France campaigned on the idea of new citizenship,' defined as one that is no longer just the preserve of nationals but open to everyone, French people and foreigners, who request it on grounds of residence.

Local participation also makes the concept of citizenship the very opposite of exclusion, illustrating its social aspect without taking away its political and legal aspect. But the demand for citizenship in Germany is linked to rights – to permanent residence, protection against racism and equality in the political arena. So citizenship becomes a way to guarantee residence, not ensure cultural integration.

In both countries there is a difference between the notion of foreigners or immigrants and their actual presence. First, the relevant social policies in France aim to integrate foreign workers and their families, while in Germany they are presented as 'policies about foreigners' (*Ausländerpolitik).* The French state gets involved with the associations, while the German authorities simply encourage foreigners to organise themselves (*Selbsthilfe*) into associations. The idea is that foreigners should set up their own organizations to combat delinquency, poverty and crime. This is similar to American liberalism, where voluntary groups in an ethnic community also provide aid and welfare for its members and focus on the community's special social problems, with the key difference that members of an ethnic group in the US have citizenship. In Germany, this system of a structured and integrated ethnic community running its own affairs implies a simultaneous struggle for recognition of equal rights that is the essence of citizenship.

So just as in France, the frontiers of 'us' can blend with the interests of the political community as soon as there is a battle to be fought against racism and exclusion, in Germany the demand for citizenship as a right of protection leads foreigners and Germans to entrench themselves in their own positions. In France, the political engagement of immigrant groups in the national community occurs through the transition from civil participation, as seen inside the various community groups, to civic participation which is expressed by the act of voting. This is a passage from a citizenship hitherto characterised by limited commitment to community-type institutions to one that manifests itself through the law that incorporates them directly in the political community.

In Germany, the requirements for getting nationality have led campaigners to devise compensation strategies which, rather than dismiss integration, seek indirect ways to obtain it. Lack of electoral weight is made up for at local level by a form of citizenship based mostly on its social practice, by setting up groups of foreigners who work out a relationship with the central government or provincial administration. The Constitutional Court's 1989 annulment of foreigners' right to vote in local elections, granted in 1987 by the Hamburg parliament, on grounds that, as in France, only the possession of nationality gave the right to vote at local or federal level, continued to keep 'blood foreigners' outside the electorate. But at local level, as in France,[18] involvement of foreigners began with setting up bodies such as advisory boards for foreigners (*Ausländerbeiräte)* in the mid-1970s and 'extra-municipal town commissions for foreigners'.

These bodies enable 'non-nationals,' as the German authorities called them, to commit themselves to 'the public good' of the town or city and raise issues with the town authorities that concern everyone, such as schools, nurseries, parks and businesses. Independent lists of candidates for election to them spark strong rivalry and sometimes even racial tension in a town, as well as within or between community associations. But the existence of candidates, especially Turks, shows a will to take part in democratic life so as to get better representation.

But the purely symbolic power of such councils means their elected members have no influence on decisions made by the town authorities. They simply present to them problems that business-people or foreign students are having or report on deficiencies in services for immigrants. But there is huge interest in elections to these councils. In Bamberg in autumn 1994, for example, 48.5 per cent of all foreigners voted to elect the local advisory council, while 78 per cent voted among Turks, four of whom were elected to the council.[19]

In France, a similar procedure has been set up, with 'extra-municipal councils' and 'associate councillors' to serve non-citizens. Despite being just as advisory and symbolic as their German counterparts, these councillors vote as full nationals do, participate in debates about foreigners in the town, appoint spokespersons, campaign for equal rights for all and are proud of appearing in the minutes of the meetings.

[18] Article 3 of the French Constitution says that 'electors are all French adult nationals of either sex with civil and civic rights.'

[19] *Cf.* L. Yalçin-Heckmann, *The Perils of Ethnic Associational Life in Europe: Turkish Migrants In Germany and France,*' paper submitted to the workshop Culture, Communication and Discourse: Negotiating Difference in Multi-Ethnic Alliances, organised by the ICCCR, Universities of Manchester and Keele, 9-12 December 1995.

So taking part in broad institutions in which 'civic virtues' are supposedly instilled leads to an effective involvement in national political life. It signals the start of exercising citizenship, which gives a person pride in being part of established local or national institutions that represent their members' interests. This new identity as a citizen results from a process of 'political acculturation' as Habermas[20] puts it – the internalization of the host country's values and the rules of its politics. Also important is the socialization at school of the younger generation, that Turkish member of the Bundestag Cem Ozdemir calls the 'new natives' (*neuer Inländer*) who he says 'have tasted the freedom of urban civil society and go their own way, resisting parental pressure and outside influences, and are totally immersed in the local culture (*Bildungsinländer* – people formed from the inside)'.[21] In such cases of virtual citizenship, acquiring German nationality is not just a right but a duty.

Citizenship expressed through both community and national institutions goes against the traditional views of 'republican' citizenship which combines political involvement and national feeling and is systematically linked to the nation-state, where its political and identity aspects are merged. But whether citizenship is political, legal, social or economic and its content cultural, legal or tied to identity, this combination amounts to a feeling of loyalty to the group, the community, civil society and the state. The strategies of the players can be seen in how these elements are interwoven. In France, an increasingly collective strategy expressed through voting and in Germany a strategy that is collective too but compensatory, where a citizen's identity does not make him 'a spectator who votes,' as Rousseau put it, but a player who seeks to influence voting by bringing pressure to bear on public opinion or government decisions.

In France, although the strategy of the players is more and more collective and the notion of citizenship now involves awareness of a special identity, people can also take part as individuals in the political community, largely because it is easier to obtain nationality than in Germany. There, despite strong participation in associations and in elections for advisory councils in some towns, the status of nationalities produces greater political isolation of 'non-Germans'. Inclusion in the system and the strong political involvement of associations does not mean inclusion in the civic community. Beyond that, the advisory councils, as the only representation non-nationals have in the towns, tend to maintain the separation. The result is an amalgam of foreigners whose division into various nationalities creates new fragmentation that keeps each national group in its own milieu. So citizenship as identity and commitment is confined to the small group, without access to the wider political community and without ties to the local community and other foreigners.

'Social citizenship' that includes the foreigner in the broader system means, at that level, direct participation in civil society, but such participation is only indirect where true political citizenship is concerned. Only 'legal' citizenship

[20] J. Habermas, 'Immigration et chauvinisme du bien-être,' *in Revue Nouvelle,* n° 10, 1992.
[21] Interview with C. Ozdemir, a Green member of the Bundestag.

carries the right to take full part in the political community. Its link with an identity that is sought after raises the issue of recognition and representativity.

Citizenship and recognition

The question of citizenship is all the more important for being tied to that of recognition.[22] Demand for recognition aims to allow groups with a special identity to escape their political marginalization and become fully part of the state. From this standpoint it is a fight for emancipation. But unlike the emancipation of the Enlightenment that separated religion from public function and the individual from the community to ensure priority identification with the national community, the demand for recognition in this case arises from a wish to take part with equal rights to be granted to religious or community identities within the state system.

In France, campaigning through associations has led to a clear collective strategy of integrating youngsters of Maghreb origin. This policy, which puts the 'I' into the 'us' in relation to the authorities, draws its strength from the fight against racism and against the National Front, which has made them a target, a fight that has made it a duty to demonstrate together. The 'us' is just a way of standing out among the French electorate. In the 1988 presidential election, 'a new kind of equation was emerging between Le Pen voters, registering on the electoral rolls and the '*beur*' vote (second generation immigrants from the Maghreb)'.[23] Militants talk about 'the republic' and universal values, but their involvement is affirmation of a group identity shared by individuals grappling with the same social problems, perceived and proven as stemming from their national origin and establishment of an ethnicity based on the same things.

Recognition of a truly shared identity is mixed up with Islam. Since the 1990s, local authority policies towards Maghreb communities have been based mainly on fear of Islam. Debate about possible incompatibility of republican citizenship and belonging to another religious or national (ethnic) identity and about incompatibility between Islam and secularism puts Islam and the Mahgreb population in France at the centre of demands for recognition. Affirmation of Islam, like emergence of an ethnicity already taking shape through certain kinds of political participation, contrasts with the doctrine of a culturally-unified nation of citizens sharing an identity. This principle of unity tries to mask any cultural, regional, linguistic or other public difference.

This applies even more to religion. But the rallying of politicians in the 'headscarf affair' (first in 1989 and then 1994) to the cause of French secularism as the pillar of social cohesion, brought Islam to the heart of the collective identification of the Maghreb immigrant population. The separation of Church and State gives legal institutional status to the Roman Catholic clergy, the National

[22] *Cf.* Ch. Taylor, *Multiculturalism and the Politics of Recognition*, Princeton University Press 1992.

[23] F. Dazi, R. Leveau, 'L'intégration par la politique, le vote des beurs,' *in Etudes*, September 1988.

Federation of Protestant Churches and to the Jews, whose status was established by the Consistory set up by Napoleon. Such recognition shows a respect for freedom of worship and the neutrality of the secular state. What place Islam should have in French society brings back into the debate the old duality between religion and the state and raises the question of giving Islam the same recognition the other religions won a century earlier. Recognition of Islam today involves a general review of the place of religions in the public arena that challenges the notion of republican secularism and how it works, along with the link between the state and religion in France.

Such recognition would be very important. It has to do, among other things, with the size of the Muslim electorate, even though it is sociologically and politically diverse. If not, how do we explain the surprising absence from the 1995 presidential campaign of talk about the remoteness of Islam as a cultural or political system described at election times as community-based? Quite simply because cultural and political acculturation have advanced, because the image of a group of French citizens who are Muslims is gaining ground even if it does not manifest itself in such terms. The issue is important enough to have revived public debate about the criteria for granting nationality.

In Germany, the demand for recognition is tied in a complicated way to the status of an ethnic minority based on a national Turkish identity and on a Muslim religious identity, both of them perceived as foreign to German collective identity. The national minority is defined by its foreign legal status and the religious minority by the marginalization of Islam compared with other religions, which have an official status. The Turks' demand for recognition has increased however as a result of the spectacular racist attacks in Germany since 1990 which have put the issue at the centre of the debate as a right to protection against 'hatred of foreigners' (*Ausländerfeindlichkeit*). The problem is that the demand for this right once more comes up against the question of legal citizenship which emphasises the legal aspect and leaves out the issue of identity. The next step would be acceptance of dual nationality which would meet head-on the German Basic Law with its blending of citizenship and nationality and become a bone of contention that would have to be negotiated.

But the demand of the Turks for dual nationality introduces clear distinctions between nationality, citizenship and identity. Citizenship (*Staatsbürgerschaft*) and nationality (*Staatsangehörigkeit*) are both linked to the state, but the first as a system and the second as belonging. Reference to dual nationality is based on this. The minority in question shows a desire to join the political community by seeking citizenship and also expresses its attachment to the nationality of origin.

Such ambiguities have been reinforced, especially by euphemistic descriptions of foreigners who have settled on national soil – from the 'non-Germans' of the conservative right and the 'foreign fellow-citizens' of the Greens. The two expressions illustrate the link, or absence of one, that some people would like to make or break between citizens and nationals. Debate centres on requirements for citizenship which leads in turn to rethinking the notion of the state and its relationship to how the nation is defined. By claiming dual nationality,

Turkish nationals see citizenship as a legal means to win political representation, and nationality as an ethnic identity, one quite similar to the identity Germans conceive for themselves. The status of minority ultimately keeps respective identities separate and debate about dual nationality ends up by defining it as a dual identity.

But granting German nationality forces Germans to recognise the immigrants have come to stay and granting dual nationality to recognise them with all the ethnic-national and religious differences that go with it. For German politicians, this means discarding the official line that Germany is not a country of immigration and accepting that Germany, like other European countries, is now a country of immigration where more than six million foreigners live in peace. Only if this is accepted can the 'non-German' population, already living for several generations in West Germany, hope to win political representation.

For the foreigners, only citizenship has a chance of putting an end to racist behaviour towards them, in that only the right to vote can influence political decisions. The political influence of the Turks in Germany is making itself felt in civil society. Apart from the impact of their community associations on public opinion, they also have significant economic weight.[24] A 1991 report published in Brussels put the direct or indirect contribution of the Turks to the German economy at around 57 billion DM – far more than the 16 billion DM[25] the welfare state spends on foreigners. In 1992, there were 35,000 Turkish businessmen, from restaurateurs to industrialists, employing a total of 150,000 Turks and 75,000 Germans and whose annual turnover was 25 billion DM and who paid one billion DM in taxes in 1991.[26]

These economical actors are not only important in relations between Germany and Turkey but also have in their hands the fate of German investments in the Turkish-speaking republics of the former Soviet Union. Statistics regularly show the scale of their investment and consumption. In France, the figures reflect the laws of citizenship and do not allow such a clear view of the immigrant population's contribution. When people get French nationality, they are classified as 'French by acquisition' and become statistically invisible. This shows the different levels, even different concepts of integration in the two countries.

But in Germany, can security based on economic presence make up for the political insecurity of not having the right to protection? Can economical integration pave the way to political rights? History has a partial response. In the 19th century, the leaders of the German economy managed to draw the country into international economic competition during the Great Depression of 1873-96.

[24] *Cf.* M. Walzer, 'The Civil Society Argument,' *in* E. Laclau & C. Mouffe (eds.) *Dimensions of Radical Democracy,* Verso 1992, pp. 89-108.

[25] *Migration News Sheet,* Brussels, December 1991, quoted in *The Economic and Political Impact of Turkish Migration in Germany,* Zentrum für Türkeistuden, March 1993.

[26] Data from the Turkish Business Association, Berlin. See also Zentrum für Türkeistuden, *Konsumgewohnheiten und wirtschaftliche situation der türkischen Bevölkerung in der Bundesrepublik Deutschland,* Essen, September 1992.

This was the base from which they grew and came to influence national political decisions.

Similarly, groups like the Turkish doctors' association since 1990 and more recently business associations in the different *Länder* are now acting as pressure groups negotiating on behalf of the Turkish community, from defending social and cultural rights to action against racism. Recalling the part played by the economy in redefining German identity after World War II, they are using their economic success to transform themselves into a political force. They take care not to present themselves as victims and try to highlight their contribution to German society and thereby earn the respect of the German authorities.

'The hard core of Germany's identity is the economy,' says Barbara John, Berlin's commissioner for immigrants (*Ausländerbeauftragte*).[27] Is she referring to the 'economic miracle' that, through prosperity and well-being, gives new meaning to the country's identity beyond the old ethnic yardstick? Or does this approach replace the meaning of citizenship with another, just as traditional one linked to the medieval status of the town-dweller (*Bürger)*? In Germany, this second vision of citizenship has more to do with belonging to a civil society than with allegiance to the political community. Civil society is understood as a bourgeois society (*die bürgerlische Gesellschaft*) that is not just separate from the state and its institutions but confronts them. In this sense, anyone who takes part in public life dominated by economic competition can be considered a citizen.

'This suggests that citizen and bourgeois, two sides of the same coin,' says Ralf Dahrendorf.[28] This is the way we should perhaps understand the term *ausländische Mitbürger* (foreign fellow-citizens) that the Greens introduced into the public arena. It means absorbing the Turks into German society through economic citizenship if it cannot be done through political citizenship. Would their attainment of bourgeois status be a step towards naturalization, as implied in the German word *Einbürgerung,* even though it refers to the state (*Staatsbürger*) and not the city, as in the case of the bourgeois?

This very special notion of citizenship puts the economy over politics, unlike in France, where politics takes precedence over the economy, at least in political discourse. But it gives the Turks in Germany, who are de facto citizens, more political weight than the Maghreb population in France, even though the latter are legally citizens, especially the younger generation. In Germany, children and grandchildren of Turkish immigrants identify with the wider society because of the success of their parents, grandparents or other Turks, seeing each as a source of ethnic pride. In France, immigration is part of the debate about social exclusion and the situation in city suburbs, whose inhabitants feel devalued and angry. In Germany, an image of economic success earns negotiating power and is seen as legitimising the claim for dual citizenship.

The refusal to incorporate 'non-German' national or religious groups into the political community underlines once more how the German nation see itself in

[27] Interview with author.

[28] R. Dahrendorf, *The Modern Social Conflict. An Essay on the Politics of Liberty,* University of California Press 1988, p. 34.

a special way. Identification with an ethnic community only has its place in civil society, where there is citizenship. The right to share in exercising political power through legal citizenship is still to be won. The dual nationality sought by the Turks is based on an approach that would link nationality to identity and citizenship to a right to indeed negotiate an ethnic-national legal personality referring both to German civil society by residence (with the rights and duties involved in that) and to Turkish nationality (for those who want it) in terms of identity, which leads to building a national minority. This ethnical identification, expressed through being a minority, is the key to the citizenship to be negotiated.

Conclusion

Building a nation-state is a process of assimilation in itself that involves establishing the principles that will match cultural and identity frontiers with territorial and political ones. The nation, that imagined or invented community, chooses its methods of inclusion and exclusion according to its idea of itself. The same goes for the relationship the two countries have today with immigrants, which is determined by steady national integration. So the participation and political involvement of the immigrant population in France and Germany are visibly part of a historical continuity of the role of the state in France and of civil society in Germany.

But in both countries the degrees of belonging and political involvement show one exercise of citizenship is separate from a notion tied only to national identity. In France, the idea of citizenship replaces in a way the notion of 'civilization,' a memory of greatness no longer shared by everyone or in the same way. When publicly linked to the phenomenon of exclusion, the notion of citizenship seems very much like an act of social compensation by politics and the law. In Germany, citizenship is mainly limited to active participation in civil society and fulfils its political function without any legal aspect. So taking part in a 'republican' political community in France, while in Germany civil society is more involved, challenges the definition and exercise of citizenship – in France citizenship against social exclusion, (as in the United States) and in Germany citizenship in favour of political inclusion.

But citizenship as civic participation no longer always theoretically rules out expression of collective identities, even if that encroaches on republican principles. New ethnical identifications, in religious or national terms, become an element of citizenship to be negotiated. This means deciding the degree of difference that is acceptable. Recognition of a national minority, which the Turks are seeking in Germany, would maintain separate identities and the lack of a right to citizenship would widen the gap and so stretch the meaning of democracy itself.

But recognition of a Muslim religious minority in France, with some citizens expressing their attachment to Islam, would not clash, empirically or in principal, with secularism, understood as the neutrality of the state in religious matters. In fact official recognition might allow Islam to develop within the framework of representative institutions far from the influence of the country of origin. However, non-recognition would raise the issue of equality between different religions in France and their representation. In Germany too, recognition of Islam would be part of the already institutionalised religious pluralism that nearly all Turkish immigrants could feel part of. And in both countries, a balance has to be struck between civil society and the state or a link made between cultural diversity and citizenship that does not undermine civic principles or the ultimate identity of the group.

This approach goes beyond a notion of citizenship as being strictly confined to the nation-state and leads to dissociation of citizenship and nationality, reducing the first to political rights and makes the second a matter of simple identity that grows and takes shape during negotiations for its recognition. The multitudes of cultural, ethnic and religious identifications and allegiances that shifts the frontiers between what is seen as private and public, which in France stems from the relationship between State and religion and in Germany the relationship between State and citizenship.

The building of Europe makes the relationship between culture and politics more vague. Just like the tactics and strategies of collective immigrant identities seeking their place in the community, the efforts and negotiations sponsored by states about the ideologies and founding myths of a nation can be seen as individual ones in the context of a united Europe. If negotiations boost feelings of identity, does that reduce a nation to a community itself in relation to communities established in reaction to hostility by nations? The tactics of states are challenged by plans for new areas of negotiation involving all national and religious communities that are helping to build a European identity.

Chapter 8

Muslims and Citizenship in the United Kingdom

Danièle Joly and Karima Imtiaz

Introduction

At all levels of society, there is widespread acceptance that there is and should be, no contradiction between being Muslim and being a British citizen. The Government's Foreign and Commonwealth Office (FCO) in its booklet *Muslims in Britain* stresses that:

> '...developing mutual respect and understanding between the different communities within Britain is seen as vital for achieving good relations between them. Britain is committed to ensuring equal opportunities for all her citizens, irrespective of their colour, race or religion. Neither Muslims, nor any other group for that matter, are expected to set aside their faith or their traditions: the Government believes that everyone should have a sense of belonging to Britain, whatever their origins. The Muslim community has wholeheartedly embraced this principle.'

This quote poses many questions: what does British citizenship mean? why should religion, and specifically Islam, have any relationship to British citizenship? how do 'equal opportunities for all her citizens, irrespective of their... religion' work in practice? who are the Muslims in Britain? What is the 'sense of belonging to Britain' for Muslims, and is this different for different groups within the Muslim population? what are the criteria and evidence that the Muslim community has embraced the principle of belonging to Britain?

Citizenship

Citizenship in the UK has these rights framed within a specific historical context – the legacy of empire, of importance to those who originated or whose forebears originated in the former colonies and who had Commonwealth citizen status, that is, the majority of Muslims in Britain - and a context of church-state relations, with an established church whose power is enshrined in constitutional legislation. The Muslim population in Great Britain is in a unique situation in Europe as regards its civil and political rights. In accordance with the 1948 law on nationality, valid until

1983, any person born on the territory of the United Kingdom and its colonies has British citizenship, and any citizen of the Commonwealth, also called a British subject (since the Queen of England is also the Queen of the Commonwealth) had the opportunity to register as a British citizen after one year's residence in the UK.

Special arrangements were made to allow Pakistanis to keep these rights after 1972 (when Pakistan left the Commonwealth) as long as they had resident status before 1973. Moreover, until 1983 *jus soli* (the principle that nationality is based on one's place of birth) automatically granted British nationality to anyone born on UK territory. Since the majority of Muslims come from the Commonwealth they therefore enjoyed the same civil and political rights as British nationals: the right to vote in all elections, the right to stand as candidate in local and general elections, the right to serve in a jury and to work in the civil service. In short, all legal political activities are open to them without restriction.

From this, there follow two important points: the majority of Muslims, being Commonwealth citizens and then, under the 1981 British Nationality Act, having the right to become full British Citizens, have always had the possibility to influence legislation through the democratic process and to exercise the same rights regarding freedom of association as other citizens. This has meant that there is also a political culture amongst Muslims whose family origins were in the Indian sub-continent of participation in politics in Britain, particularly, but not exclusively, local politics.

Great Britain is a Protestant Christian society, not only in its history and its traditions but also in its state structures: the Queen is officially both head of the Anglican church (the Church of England) - and has the title 'Defender of the Faith' on the coinage - and head of state. Even though real powers are devolved to the Archbishop of Canterbury and to the Prime Minister, the non-separation of church and state permeates all levels of British life. For example, there is still a law against blasphemy, which is aimed at protecting the Christian religion. The 1944 and 1988 education laws make religious instruction obligatory and require that the school day begins with collective prayer of a Christian nature (1988). In the courts of law, oaths are sworn on the Bible, and meetings of the town council start with a prayer. Anglican pastors have the power to celebrate marriages which are automatically legal, without going through the register office. Moreover, certain religious minorities like Roman Catholics and Jews have secured an officially recognised space for themselves, with the right to celebrate marriages recognised in law, for example, or the right to obtain state funding for their schools. In other words, religion enjoys full rights within British public life. It is to be expected that this will give Muslims moral and legal justification in support of their demands and, in theory at least, better chances of success (Joly, 1989b). But the Muslims will probably feel all the more indignant and determined to pursue action if it appears openly that they are not treated on an equal footing with the other religions mentioned above.[1]

[1] In 1998 the law on the registration of marriages was changed, so that now, a far wider range of buildings, for example, hotels and historic buildings,can be used for the solemnization of marriages,with the registrar coming out to the building. This, however, is

Secondly, within a state dominated by the Anglican Church, Muslims have been able, as have other religious minorities such as Quakers, Roman Catholics and Jews, to have their distinct needs covered by legislation (see Modood, 1997). In some cases, they have benefited from the struggles of these 'earlier' religious minorities. Areas where this is significant and/or symbolic are: freedom to attend university without a religious test' and therefore, access to the professions;[2] freedom, subject to planning permission, to construct places of worship and not to pay tax on these buildings; permission to run their own schools (although as will be seen later, parity of state funding is a major Muslim demand); permission to have *halal* slaughtering, just as Jews have kosher slaughtering[3] right to swear in court on the religious book of one's own faith, or simply to affirm;[4] the custom, although not a legal right, that schools and employers will allow those of minority faiths some of their religious holidays, albeit unpaid or taken out of their annual leave; and provision for marriages and burials. As will be seen later, Muslims have often settled in the areas of cities formerly inhabited by Jews or Catholics, leading to interesting situations, particularly in the field of education (see Catholic Bishop's Conference, 1997). In certain instances, such as prison, hospitals and even university chaplaincy services and in civic religion (e.g. ceremonies that mark the beginning of a local council's new year of business, or remembrance Day services and parades, commemorating those who died in war) the Christian clergy are those who actually facilitate the participation of other faiths (see Beckford & Gilliat, 1996).

Demographic profile and geographical distribution of Muslims

It cannot be too highly emphasised that all the large-scale statistical information about Muslims has been gathered from a point of view of ethnicity[5] rather than religious affiliation and practice as such, and so is fundamentally flawed. Nevertheless, over 90 per cent of people from Pakistan and Bangladesh, plus their descendants, can be assumed to be Muslims, although there are growing numbers of British converts of all ethnicities and now second-generation Muslims of white and African-Caribbean ethnicity. The oldest Muslim communities in Britain (see

costly and may be why Muslims have continued to have a registry office ceremony in addition to celebrating the Nikkah in the mosque.

[2] Even today, Oxford University, in its Prospectus, feels it necessary to emphasize that admission is open to all who fit the academic criteria, regardless of religion.

[3] It is interesting to note that Muslim *halal* butchers, just like Jewish kosher butchers, are only supposed to sell meat to other Muslims and Jews, presumably to avoid allegations of unfair competition. In practice, this law in unenforceable. For more information, see Nielsen, 1992 and 1995.

[4] Most Muslims opt to sear on the Qur'an. However, the Salafis, who are a very small minority, like Quakers, have a theological objection to swearing on the Holy Book and so would opt to affirm.

[5] As pointed out before, the main source of national statistical information has come from answers to the 'ethnicity question' in the 1991 Census. The 2001 census will have a question on religion, which will enable much more accurate profiles to be built up.

the FCO video, Islam in Britain), however, are those who settled in seaports such as Cardiff, Liverpool, and South Shields in the mid-nineteenth century, that is the Yemenis (see Halliday, 1992) and the Somalis (in more recent years, the numbers of the latter have been increased by refugees and asylum-seekers). Two cities with significant proportions of Pakistanis are Birmingham (13.9 per cent of all British Pakistanis) and Bradford (9.5 per cent of British Pakistanis). In these cities, people of Pakistani and Bangladeshi origin are not evenly distributed geographically. In a few wards in several cities, they constitute the biggest single ethnic group, which has important implications in terms of local politics. For example, areas in which the proportion of voters could have made a difference in an election - assuming voting along 'ethnic' lines are: Birmingham Sparkbrook, with 27.7 per cent of the electorate being Pakistani, Bethnal Green and Bow in east London, where 27.51 per cent were Bangladeshi, Bradford West, with 26.17 per cent Pakistani, Birmingham Ladywood at 15.57 per cent Pakistani, Rochdale and also Bradford North both at just over 11 per cent Pakistani voters, and Poplar and Canning Town in east London at 11.15 per cent Bangladeshi voters.[6]

The only Muslims for whom we have any statistical data, however unreliable, are the Muslims from the Indian sub-continent. They are a young population, with the majority under 25, and a much smaller proportion than the white population having reached retirement age. There has been a trend for those reaching retirement age to return to live in the sub-continent, but that trend appears to be slowing now and an ageing population will its specific needs met regarding, health, welfare and social provision. As more women from the Muslim minority communities go to work outside the home, so provision for the Muslim elderly in terms of day care centres and even residential accommodation will become more important. Amongst Pakistani women, fertility rates appear to be dropping and there is a trend towards the British average. This is less the case with Bangladeshi women (see Ballard and Kalra, 1994: 14-15). We can assume that, as fertility rates drop, so women's economic activity outside the home will increase proportionately. Childcare in terms of nurseries and before and after school provision will therefore become increasingly important. Of major concern is that a small number of economically active people are supporting a relatively large number of children, students, non-working spouses, elderly and sick relatives and other non-economically active household members. This must inevitably put a strain on the working members of the household which will have its results in terms of ill-health in later life. Indeed, in terms of being permanently removed from the labour force for reasons of permanent sickness, Ballard and Kalra (1994: 38-9) found that Bangladeshi men were the highest of all ethnic groups at 9 per cent and Pakistanis second at just over 8 per cent. They comment: 'While the Census figures themselves offer no explanation as to just why that should be so, it is worth remembering that before the recession of the early eighties decimated

[6] These figures are taken from the *Islamophobia report* (Table 2, p. 14), whose source for this information was the Ethnic Minority Data Archive, University of Warwick. The table is headed: 'The constituencies in which voters of Pakistani and Bangladeshi origin constituted at least eight percent of the electorate in the 1997 general election.'

manufacturing industry, Pakistanis and Bangladeshis were particularly concentrated in heavy manual, unpleasant, low-paid industrial jobs. The Census figures would seem to show not only that members of these groups were particularly vulnerable to redundancy followed by long-term unemployment, but to severe health problems as well.' (Ballard & Kalra,1994:38).

Patterns of deprivation

Tariq Modood, speaking at one of the talks organized by Birmingham City Council in the summer of 1997 (Equalities Division, 1997:21-22) said of research done by this team at the Policy Studies Institute

'Of the six groups we studied we found that actually they fell into roughly speaking three broad bands. The Pakistanis and Bangladeshis were really very, very disadvantaged by any measure that you could think of. Unemployment levels, earnings, the kind of jobs people were in, the kind of qualifications people had, household income, housing and health (you name it we used a whole battery of measures) and the picture was always the same - the Pakistanis and Bangladeshis were easily the most disadvantaged groups. I don't actually mean the most disadvantaged ethnic groups, they were more disadvantaged than other groups formed by other social processes. So, for instance, looking at household income, one would expect pensioner households and lone parent households to be the two most disadvantaged in terms of income per household, but Pakistanis and Bangladeshis were below them.'

Those in the 'second band' were people of Caribbean and Indian origin, of whom Modood says: '...they clearly were experiencing a socio-economic disadvantage relative to the white population, but it was not of such a severe kind as for the Pakistanis and Bangladeshis' (1997:22). In the 'third band' came the Chinese and African-Asians, 'who, again speaking in general terms in terms of job levels, earnings, access to higher education and so on, were on a par with the white population' (1997:22). Again, it must be stressed that Muslims can be found in any of these broad ethnic minority groupings, as well as within the white majority. In addition, and most significantly for the future, where Pakistanis at least outstrip all other ethnic groups, including the white majority, is in continuing their education after 16 and subsequently, at 18 or 19, in studying at university. Another aspect in which Pakistanis outstrip other ethnic groups is that they are owner occupiers of their homes, rather than tenants – for more information, see the section on Birmingham, below.

Table 1. Economic position for Pakistani Residents – Great Britain (residents 16+)[7]

Economic position	All Residents	Pakistani
Economically active	61.04	50.96
In employment	90.72	71.22
Employees – full time	68.13	63.53
Employees – part-time	17.75	9.16
Self-employed –with employees	4.30	8.78
On a government scheme	1.45	4.48
Unemployed	9.28	28.78
Permanently sick	10.53	11.54
Retired	48.06	6.67
Students	38.96	49.04
Other inactive	31.00	58.95

All major studies have shown even higher levels of economic inactivity amongst Bangladeshis than Pakistanis, slightly higher levels in the permanently sick category, fewer as students, lower household income, and worse housing conditions (forthcoming Owen). Although the levels of self-employment for both Pakistanis and Bangladeshis appear to augur well – and indeed, many from the communities are proud of the independence self-employment represents – it tends to be concentrated in certain service sectors, such as catering and taxi-driving.

There is an argument that the high levels of self-employment are in part, a reaction by Bangladeshis and Pakistanis to the discrimination they face in the jobs market. Modood comments:

We asked all the minority groups whether they had experienced racial discrimination in employment, and, if they did what in their opinion was it about them that led to the rejection – to the refusal of a job... roughly about half of South Asians said it was their race. We also asked them if they thought it was their religion. The point I want to make is that about 40 per cent of South Asians thought that religion and race combined together in the racial discrimination they had personally experienced. (Equalities Division, 1997:26).

Given this perception, it is not hard to see why Muslims and Islamic organizations believe that the Race Relations laws are inadequate to protect Muslims against discrimination, whatever their ethnic origins.

[7] This information is from Birmingham City Council's publication Community Profiles – Pakistani, p. 2 and is taken from the 1991 Census.

Politics, community formation and British Muslims

Muslims in Britain are operating in a particular context with a particular history of imperial relations and Church/State relations (see Modood, 1997). The British Raj in India (and it is In the Indian sub-continent that the majority of British Muslims have their origins) had policies that were simultaneously 'divide and rule' and about using local structures and forming communities to work through. The Indian battalions of the British Army, for instance, were divided along lines of religion and caste, thus reinforcing those divisions. They also sought to build up a strong identity based on region of recruitment. These identities helped ensure an 'esprit de corps' and psychologically deterred a man from showing any 'cowardice' in battle in front of his fellows. As in military life, it was the case in civilian life - although there was considerable overlap, as the armed forces provided cradle-to-grave support for their members in the form of schools, colleges, hospitals, housing on a 'compound' with all community facilities, pensions, and graveyards. Many of these identities have persisted post-independence. In addition, the British used local structures and native legal systems, with some adaptations, as a means of forging the institutions of rule. As we have seen above, Islam pursues exactly the same policy, which works well in an imperial situation. So, for instance, there was Muslim Personal Law in the Indian colonial state. Today, the demand for Muslim Personal Law to be instituted in Britain for Muslims comes from Muslims with sub-continental origins, such as Khurshid Ahmed of the Islamic Foundation and the authors of the book on the Rushdie Affair, Ahsan and Kidwai. Most other British Muslims who are legal scholars, such as Ahmed Andrews of the Association of Muslim Lawyers and the late Sebastian Poulter, favour adaptations to British law to eliminate any residual discrimination against Muslims and for wider use of European law. This appears to be becoming reality. This history means that both the British rulers and the Muslim subjects became accustomed to ways of operating, which have been transplanted to mainland Britain and continue into the twenty-first century. These include a concentration on local community; an acceptance of custom and practice into common law; the use of gate-keepers and community leaders. Much community formation is facilitated by the fact that, in Britain, it is very easy to form a community association, just as it is very easy and cheap to start a business - and Muslims are self-employed and owners of small businesses out of all proportion to their numbers.

Immigration and settlement patterns have meant that though there are Muslims in most towns and cities in Britain, in a few cities, notably Birmingham and Bradford, and certain areas of east London such as Tower Hamlets, they are very concentrated in certain areas and in certain electoral wards. This is very important, as Britain does not have proportional representation but a 'first past the post' voting system for both national and local elections. Hence, the concentration of Muslims has to be very important if they are to have a political voice through the ballot box. According to figures quoted in the *islamophobia* Report (1997: 14, Tables 1, 2) there is a sufficient proportion of Pakistanis and Bangladeshi voters in two constituencies to make a difference in voting outcomes in Birmingham, Sparkbrook and Ladywood; one in London, Bethnal Green and Bow; and in

Bradford and Bradford West. These tables also show that 13.9 per cent of British Pakistanis live in Birmingham, and 9.5 per cent in Bradford. Making a difference in voting outcomes of course presupposes that the Pakistani and Bangladeshi voters will unite behind one candidate - and this did not happen in Bradford West in the last general election, where the vote was split, and Masha Singh, a Sikh, was elected. In Sparkbrook, the running of the local constituency Labour Party had been taken from local control and a candidate was imposed by the party's national executive. In consequence, a white, non-Muslim was elected, even though most party activists are of Pakistani origin, as are several local councillors. The only Muslim elected MP in the general election was Mohammed Sarwar in Glasgow, where, according to the *Islamophobia* figures, 2.3 per cent of British Pakistanis live. Clearly Sarwar had a wide, trans-ethnic appeal. A socialist and a millionaire, a former trade unionist, he is also a significant local employer. Nevertheless, his time as MP has not been without controversy. For almost a year, he was suspended by the Labour Party whilst investigations regarding bribery took place. Eventually he was cleared, but many questioned whether a white, non-Muslim MP would have been treated in this way (see the *British Muslims Monthly Survey*).

Mode of social organization, mobilization and demands

Associational life is dominated by religious institutions. Indeed, it is the mosques and the Islamic associations that mostly determine the way in which Muslim populations are incorporated into the host society. There are many mosques, and many different kinds of mosque. There may be almost 1,000 mosques in Great Britain, but the figures are only approximate because new mosques are appearing all the time. Communities and mosques complement and strengthen each other. The moral and religious conduct of each individual is monitored by the community, whilst the mosques, supported by the networks, help to restructure and reinforce religious beliefs. Islam as *din* ('way of life') governs not only moral practice, but also social relations, marriage, divorce, family relationships, economic and political affairs and even the most mundane acts of daily life.

A distinction must be made between two types of mosque (Joly, 1987). First of all, small district mosques were set up following the first stage of immigration. They are based in private houses, and the followers reflect a fairly homogeneous ethnic and theological base. In each district, there are several small mosques, and sometimes more than one in the same street. Each branch of Islam will have its own mosques according to the allegiance of the local inhabitants. As it often happens that populations of different national or regional origins live in the same district, each of the groups will establish its own mosque. This type of mosque is the most common and it plays a similar role to that of the mosque in the country of origin, acting as a place of prayer and a small *madrasa* (Quranic school).

Arguably, the mosque supplements civil society by offering an Islamic space which is lacking outside the *Dar al Islam* (land of Islam), though, given impetus following the war in Bosnia, definitions of what is the Dar al Islam are being contested. Of course, its primary function is as a place of worship where the faithful gather to pray, especially on Fridays when collective prayer is obligatory for men. However, given the Christian calendar which makes Sunday and not Friday the day of rest in Great Britain, Sunday preaching and weekend rallies also attract a sizeable gathering. Often, this teaching is carried out in English so as to be understood by the second generation. The mosque is also a centre for social gathering, where hundreds or even thousands of people (depending on the capacity of the building) get together for the main religious feasts: *Eid-ul-Fitr* at the end of Ramadan, *Eid-ul-Adha* (marking Abraham's willingness to sacrifice his son, Ishmael) and the birthday of the Prophet Mohammed. The whole family attends, wearing clothes newly bought for the festival. Many mosques also have halls which can be hired for parties, such as wedding celebrations. Most mosques have a *madrasa* where children study the Quran each evening after school; where there is no mosque in an area, then classrooms in state schools are sometimes used. Teaching methods are frequently a matter of debate and controversy. In some *madrasas,* the teaching methods take account of elements of the British model. They advocate a more flexible approach and stimulate discussion with pupils, rather than teaching based solely on the teacher's authority, and sometimes recommend the use of English texts to help the study of the Quran. Many mosques/related Islamic associations also offer lessons in the language of the country of origin (such as Urdu, Bengali, Arabic, Turkish). In addition, they may house a number of services: bookshops, libraries, community centres, funeral services, marriage bureau and marriage guidance, job centres, welfare benefits advice assistance and so on. They run groups for women, young people and the elderly.

The 'new' mosques also strive to make a space for Islam within the fabric of British society. They play a mediating role between the Muslim communities and British society, either through public relations exercises (some mosques invite teachers and pupils from local schools to their ceremonies or invite priests from neighbouring churches to theological discussions) or as pressure groups, negotiating with local authorities on various issues and even launching national campaigns. The mosques' role is also influenced by their applications to local authorities for funding, which is given only for non-religious activities. In some of the poorer inner-city areas, a new mosque may be the only significant new construction planned, and so the economic planning and development department of the town council, who have a major say in the recommending or rejecting of planning applications, often see their role as a proactive one. There may well be Muslim council officials or councillors involved, too. In reality, all types of mosques have evolved to a greater or lesser extent. Some of those involved are questioning their relevance to the younger generation, especially where the mosque is in an area of multiple deprivation, and there is little or no youth provision. Many mosques belong to a network or federation corresponding to the various branches of Islam represented in Britain, but remain autonomous, rather like the smaller evangelical protestant churches.

Although a new phenomenon adapted to the situation of immigration, there are mosques that do not show any religious tendencies other than those of the country of origin. They must be seen within the perspective of a reaffirmation of a collective identity rooted in the cultural and religious heritage of the society of origin. Sometimes the word 'Pakistani' or 'Bangladeshi' features in the name of the Islamic association which has fund-raised and organized to build and manage the mosque. 'British' Islam', particularly that which centres around local mosques, still largely reflects varieties of Islam that are found in the Indian peninsula. The same is not true for large central mosques, such as the Central Mosque in Regent's Park, London, nor many groupings in universities. It is important to realize that the major division does not lie with the Shi'ite-Sunni split, in terms either of numbers or degree of hostility.

The world of the mosques in Britain is not free of conflicts, as there are occasionally disagreements between Sufis and the UK Islamic Mission, allied to the Markazi Jamiat Ahl-e-Hadith, for example, on opposing viewpoints on teaching methods (Raza, 1991). As mentioned above, some of the *imams* who use traditional methods (often quite authoritarian teaching in the parents' language) find themselves up against those who advocate discussions on the Quran in English, in order to gain the attention of children schooled in Britain, whose main language is now English. The custom of recruiting *imams* from the mosque of the native village and the shortage of *imams* trained in Great Britain have posed problems for those who wish to renovate teaching methods. This shortage is now being addressed by the *Dar al Ulooms,* whose education in their schools in Britain is trilingual, using Arabic, English and Urdu and whose British-trained graduates (many of whom also spend several years studying at Al-Azhar university in Cairo or at Riyadh University) are now working in mosques in Britain. The graduates of the Dar-ul-Uloom *Alim* (Islamic scholar) programme are also granted a concession of one or two years on the Applied Theological Studies degree course at Westhill College, University of Birmingham. There is also considerable interchange of religious scholars of all ethnicities between Britain and the USA and the opportunity for 'ordinary Muslims', both women and men, from various tendencies, to visit the USA and Canada to see different methods of religious education, both for adults and children, there. In addition, computer technology is now being applied to the teaching and learning of the Quran and other Islamic religious knowledge and CD-Roms are widely available.

One final observation should be made about mosques in Britain. Although they receive some funding from Muslim countries (Saudi Arabia, Libya and Iraq formerly, Pakistan and others), they are essentially an autonomous, autochthonous phenomenon. They are not governed by the states of origin, whose influence remains limited; their importance stems mainly from the stabilization of Muslim populations in the land of immigration.

As noted above, the vast majority of Muslims have had British nationality and all the rights associated with it since their arrival. This has equipped them with the capacity to cut through the complications of the political process and they have made good use of it. The non-separation of the Church and the state has also created a space within which they can advance Muslim demands. In short, all legal political activities are open to them without restriction.

Some laws and political measures at national level have an impact on the Muslim population. Sometimes, it is the absence of rules which has a decisive influence: for example, Muslim first names do not pose a problem because all first names are allowed in law and so no pressure is brought to bear on Muslim parents who register their new-born children. Muslims themselves, however, have occasionally put forward demands which appear to run counter to the existing law. During the 1984 general election, a Muslim charter was produced which demanded among other things that the *Sharia* should be given a place in personal law, that is, law governing marriage, divorce, childcare and inheritance. This would be impossible in Britain because the law covers everyone, even nationals of another state, in all areas. Nothing has come of these demands. But other cases of jurisprudence show that the cultural and religious specificities of Muslims are sometimes taken into account, which in Britain assumes more importance as customary law prevails and not Roman law. On two occasions, the courts have forced Muslim husbands to comply with the contract (according to the *Sharia)* which requires the payment of a dowry *(mahr)* in the case of divorce (Shahnaz v. Rizwan, 1965; Qureshi v. Qureshi, 1972). In some ways, there is a convergence of Islamic law and British law, such as the reforms of the divorce laws, which now put much more emphasis on the need for attempts at reconciliation. Other ways in which space for Muslim-friendly practices can be achieved is in the provision of housing. Since Islam forbids interest, seeing it as usury, there are Muslims who consider that they cannot buy their home on a mortgage. Changes in the interpretation of commercial law have made schemes such as the so-called 'Muslim mortgage' and Islamically-run housing co-operatives a possibility. The Association of Muslim Lawyers and individual Muslims specialising in property law have been the leaders in these fields.

There is another aspect of the British state which will have a decisive impact on the forms of its relationships with the Muslim populations: a strong decentralization of powers, despite the previous Conservative government's efforts to reduce it. Guided by general national laws, local authorities run education, social services, housing, leisure and community services, public health, economic development, urban development and equal opportunities programmes. National bodies have competence only in health - and this is waning; the Department of Health and Social Security - and important areas of budgets are managed locally; and the police, which also has an obligation to liase and consult with the local population. Consequently, most of the questions raised by Muslims will be tackled at local level, which allows more flexibility and makes it easier to adopt pragmatic solutions and compromises that avoid national confrontations in many areas. This general trend is reinforced by a political culture steeped in empirical pragmatism. The other side of the coin is a lack of homogeneity, leading to disparities between local arrangements. Schools and education are a case in point where decentralization has facilitated Muslim gains.

According to Article 11 of the 1988 Education Reform Act, each LEA (Local Eductaion Authority) must set up a SACRE, which will decide on the assembly appropriate for each school, to reflect the religious composition the school or a section of the school, at the request of the school's head. The SACRE also works closely with the local education authority's religious advisors, who advise schools on all sorts of religious and cultural aspects of the curriculum and school life. The SACRE should be composed, among others, of representatives of the various religions practised in the catchment area. In addition, the law preserves parents' rights to withdraw their children from assembly and from Christian religious education classes. Other clauses of the law are of relevance to Muslims, particularly the introduction of a national syllabus, provision for increased representation of parents on the schools' governing bodies, with greater powers, and the possibility for schools to opt out of local authority control and come directly under the control of the Ministry of Education. One interesting example of Muslims being able to take advantage of these changes is a group of three formerly Roman Catholic primary schools in Liverpool which were faced with closure due to declining numbers of Catholic children in the area. The Catholic Church has co-operated with local Muslims and the school has now "opted out" to become a school with a 'mainly Islamic ethos'.

On the whole, it appears that the situation has changed considerably in the last twenty years in the field of education. A dialogue has been built up. Confrontations and negotiations have revealed an increased flexibility on the part of LEAs, heads of schools and the Muslims themselves. Compromises have been adopted, and it looked as though several problems had been resolved or at least that a *modus vivendi* had been reached. This was largely the fruit of Muslims' mobilization and organization in furthering their demands. But these achievements were called into question at the end of the 1980s, particularly in regard to the specifically religious issues.

Birmingham case study

All the measures of deprivation which apply nationally are also true for Birmingham Pakistanis and Bangladeshis, but often the statistics conceal high levels of achievement, too. Two sources of information on these communities are Birmingham City Council's Equalities Division reports (1997), Community Profiles – Bangladeshi (referred to as CPB) and Community Profiles – Pakistani (referred to as CPP). Particularly amongst Pakistanis, participation in further and higher education, self-employment and employing others, and owning ones own house rather than renting are all at higher than average levels. These gains are obviously the fruit of hard work, what Modood (1997) has referred to as the 'Muslim work-ethic', a variant on the 'Protestant work-ethic.'

Indeed, self-help is evident at every level amongst Muslims in Birmingham. There are after-school classes coaching children so that they can pass the eleven-plus examination – Birmingham continues to have selective schools and Muslims are over – represented among these in proportion to their numbers in the population; classes to help school students achieve good results in GCSE and A-level examinations, particularly in English, Maths and the Sciences; students in the Islamic students' societies in colleges and universities helping each other in many ways, not only in spiritual matters; and flourishing associations of Muslim professionals, such as doctors and dentists and lawyers. The recently-built Ghamkolvia Mosque in Golden Hillock affectionately known as 'Sufi Abdullah's Mosque', since the inspiration of the Suf Sheikh continues to be a source of strength, has associated with it a Job Centre/JobClub, various training projects including ones specially targeted at women, and; business enterprise centre.

> 'What is quite clear is that the two religious faiths that are very strongly in favour of state funding for religious schools are the Roman Catholics and the Muslims at 42 per cent and 49 per cent respectively. Something like half the Muslims said they supported state funding for religious schools. That is not the same thing as saying I want to send my children there because we asked that question as well, and what we found is, the figures halved when it came to the question of 'if such schools were available in your area, would you send your child there?' That is to say, roughly half in every religious group who see it as an issue of principle say 'yes, that is what I want for my own child.'

Another issue which concerned Muslims was being recognized as such, rather than as members of an ethnic group. S., a community development worker of African-Caribbean origin, said:

'Birmingham has the highest number of African-Caribbean Muslims in the country and it's really growing. It's the same with whites, but we're not recognized, none of us. That's why I think there should be a Census question on religion. But, there's got to be an agreement about how that information is going to be used. There needs to be an agreement between all the Muslim associations and the government that the information will be used to benefit us, not make other people think 'fundamentalists' and terrorists'.'

S. felt strongly that Muslims were demonised in the press and that this adversely affected community relations. He said: 'It's the same fear that there's an Irish person living next door to you and that they might be a terrorist, a bomber. It doesn't make sense if people really stop and think, but they don't sometimes, they just accept stereotypes.' Interestingly, S. felt that it was religious issues such as prayer facilities at work, that were now 'on the agenda' and that mobilization around these issues and winning them would have the beneficial side-effect of convincing non-Muslims, including those in power, that Muslims are peaceful, hard-working people who simply want mutual respect from colleagues and neighbours and are not terrorists.

The need for physical space to practice the faith and to develop as communities is an on-going issue. Although many Birmingham Muslims feel that their own neighbourhood may be convenient in many ways, with mosques and madrasas and other community provision, it was felt that facilities for young people such as appropriate youth clubs, community arts facilities and outreach youth services were still inadequate. In addition, women felt that more could be done to break down the isolation that many experience, especially as mothers of young children who do not go out to work, and those suffering from depressive illness either themselves or within the family (see Clay, 1999). Again, the need for appropriate services for Muslims was stressed, where Islamic values are respected and taken into account and where Muslims themselves run the service and decide on its priorities, rather than having other-imposed definitions and ways of operating.

Conclusion

One paradox remains to be explained: while Muslims display serious patterns of deprivation and disadvantage the community as a whole has had considerable political success. There have been achievements in national politics and local politics; legal reforms; entry into the professions; the adaptation of a wide range of public services to Muslim needs; the start of state funding for Muslim schools,[8] Muslims in the media; Muslims succeeding in the arts, sports and many other high profile areas; some sensitive covering of Islamic issues on television and some limited religious broadcasting on radio and television; regular consultation with government; and symbolic gestures such as the political parties sending messages of greeting to Muslims for Ramadam and Eid and the House of Commons Eid party. These achievements have come about through political means, the actions of pressure groups – including the professional associations and the Muslim umbrella groups, lobbying, campaigning, and sensitive Muslim leadership all together, in alliance with non-Muslim activists and politicians within mainstream parties', in particular the Labour Party.

Multiculturalism, the framework in which the content of citizenship is often expressed, is promoted by local government. The more sceptical would say that this is a way of pacifying and co-opting minorities such as Muslims, nevertheless, it has become an accepted part of the British way of life. There has been a gradual acceptance in local government and other public institutions of religion in general and Islam in particular, as a legitimate category (see Samad, 1997). At national level, the government can perhaps afford to be more tolerant, not less, and as we have shown, is concerned to maintain good relations with Muslim countries, Saudi Arabia and the Gulf States in particular. There is also the sympathy of royalty for Islam, that of Prince Charles in particular, with his numerous public statements of support for the ideals of Islam and for Muslims. He is also the founder, patron and one of the sources of finance for the Prince of Wales's Foundation for Architecture and the Building Arts, VITA (Visual Islamic and Traditional Arts).

The Muslim organizations take on the characteristics of their leaders. It is perhaps significant that many of these figures are not of Pakistani or Bangladeshi origin, but are converts – not only whites but also African-Caribbeans; or Yemenis; or of Arab origins and so on. It may be that these people are perceived by their followers as well as the state as having the ability to unite a heterogeneous and

[8] To date only two Muslim schools have received state funding, one in Birmingham and one in London. This compares to 45 state-funded Jewish schools, for a Jewish population less than half the size of the Muslim population, and several thousand Church of England and Roman Catholic schools.

cosmopolitan community and to represent fairly the interests of such a diverse population, whilst also aiming for the creation of an autochthonous Islam. Indeed, the concept of a more autochthonous Islam, within a European framework, is one warmly embraced by the Islamic Foundation in Leicester. The Islamic Foundation recently invited Professor Tariq Ramadan from Switzerland to spend a sabbatical year with them in order to research and write a book on being a Muslim in Europe. Although Muslims may appear to be as insular and cut off from mainland Europe as their non-Muslim fellow citizens, there is considerable contact with mainland Europe. The Jamaat-i-Islami, who have been influential in the Islamic Foundation in the past, have strong cross-European links, as does the *daw'ah* [modernist/reform] movement, the Tablighi Jamaat. The Sufi movements have groups in many European countries and these meet together, often very informally, in Britain and elsewhere. Muslim students from other European countries are sent to study in the Deobandi schools and seminaries at Bury, Dewsbury and elsewhere in Britain. All these encounters give British Muslims an opportunity to share experiences with other European Muslims and to realize what they have in common in terms of the issues facing them. There is also a United States' dimension. Islam is the fastest-growing religion in the US, to the extent that there is predicted to soon be more Muslims than Jews. The links with the US have increased exponentially due to the popularity of the internet, particularly among young British Muslims. There are also exchanges of preachers, students and teachers between Britain and the United States and growing Islamic scholarship using the English language as its medium.

The need for more ethnographic work, hopefully complemented by the results of the religious question in the 2001 Census, has been highlighted. Of crucial importance in looking at issues of Muslims as British citizens is the situation, identity and views of the younger generation, those under thirty, paying attention to nuances of gender, class and education as well as ethnicity. This was done to a limited extent by Stopes-Roe in 1991, but her work looks at British Asians, not only British Muslim Asians, and is now more than ten years out of date. Such work needs to combine both the subjective aspect of what it means to be a British Muslim citizen, measured by attitudes, and the subjective aspects of identity, plus the more objective aspects, as measured by participation in citizenship. Birmingham would be an ideal for location for a case-study. There are concentrations of Pakistani-origin Muslims in certain areas, which, as we have already signalled, gives considerable political advantages. There are other ethnically-based communities, such as the Yemenis, whose community centre in the Bordesley area provides a meeting place for Muslims of many ethnicities and is a focus for self-help on a wide range of issues, including the aim of starting a Muslim women's telephone help and counselling service. There are mosques that are largely attended by Asian-origin Muslims, but also have considerable numbers of converts as active members. There are growing refugee populations. The city council in its changing attitudes to Muslims and incorporation of them would make a fascinating study in itself, and there are many interfaith initiatives which show some of the difficulties Muslims face as a religious minority.

Chapter 9

Promoting A Faith-based Citizenship: The Case of Tariq Ramadan

Khadija Mohsen-Finan

Over the past decade, Islam in Europe has seen big changes, with the rise of new preachers who present Islam without reference to state structures or other institutions. New, better-educated leaders have emerged, some of them with the intellectual, organisational and political skills to play a major part in the permanent settlement of Muslim immigrants. Such preachers also encourage and organise study and discussion about the place of Islam in the society.

The new leaders have established themselves through their charisma. Their power is tied to their ability to dominate, make people listen to them and influence youths who identify themselves as Muslims and are looking for meaning in their lives. Tariq Ramadan is a good example of this new leadership and message, whose authority and legitimacy is based less on mastery of religious knowledge than on personal performance and background.

His success is less due to the rigour and strictness of his message than to the absence of religious authorities and to his use of language adapted to the expectations and needs of young people who want to learn about their identity and cultural roots and how they can best be Muslims in a largely secular society.

The absence of religious authorities

Many young Muslims in Europe have shown a keen interest in Islam over the past 20 years, yet there are no recognised religious authorities to meet their needs. This lack of structure has meant religious leadership has become fragmented.

Gilles Kepel[1] says the 'demand for Islam' – as shown by the growing number of mosques since the late 1970s – stems from the realization by many Muslim immigrants that they are settling for good in the host countries. For a lot of them, this involves affirming a religious identity there by providing themselves with the means to practice their faith.

[1] G. Kepel, *Les Banlieues de l'Islam: naissance d'une religion en France*, Paris, Seuil.

For these people, who were either born in Europe or emigrated there, the problem of how to define themselves is crucial. They communicate poorly with their parents, often no longer speaking the same language or sharing the same values and standards of behaviour.

They become alienated from their families and say their parents do not understand or practise 'true Islam' and are more influenced by customs and superstition than by faith. These youngsters, who describe themselves as Muslims and stress they are 'religiously active,' are searching for a thinking universal Islam based on individual reasoning. They reject an identity based on their parents' national origin, which they no longer connect with, and also reject the label of 'Arab' or 'beur' they are often automatically given.

So they listen to the fundamentalist message, especially since the secular school system does not teach them about Islam and their parents do not tell them about it.

During the 1980s and especially the 1990s, the atmosphere in Europe, notably France, was also extremely hostile to Islam. Confusion, suspicion and stereotyping undermined the Muslim community, which retreated into self-justification on the basis of its religion and religious identity.

So efforts to represent, organize and regulate Islam in France have come up against the flaws in the way Islam operates. These mainly involve the fragmentation of a community inevitably split because of the various relationships Muslims have with their religion, but also because of their expectations of it and the absence so far of public representatives. On top of this, insufficiently or badly trained imams are funded by Arab countries and sent to control their nationals abroad.

The rise of a new kind of sermon

This situation encourages the emergence of new activists promoting an Islam adapted to life in Europe – a version unencumbered by the quarrels that have divided the community and made some youngsters withdraw into themselves because they feel humiliated, marginalized or rejected. Such new leaders offer these youths a fresh identity that transcends national, ethnic or racial points of reference, a supra-national one closer to a European, even universal order of things in tune with the image of the modern world, where national borders are unmarked and life-styles largely similar.

This message finds an audience among a minority of Muslims from immigrant families who have become alienated from their parents' culture but are worried about losing their identity if they became totally integrated into European society and effectively assimilated.

But this quest for a universal Islam, built and adapted to the host society, requires both a break with family life and adjustment of traditions to the situation the Muslim minority are living in. This is usually known as 're-islamicisation.' Such a process is not easy and needs points of reference to guide it or protect it.

So while the state wants to institutionalize Islam or organize it from above, local-level adjustments are being made through community groups and by the words and actions of preachers in effect following up the work done by religious associations. These and the preachers are occupying the void created by the flaws in the operation of Islam in France.

During the 1990s, the leadership of Islam in Europe was profoundly affected by the arrival of religious figures who have imposed their personalities on the community. Their role is different from that of the imam who acted as an intermediary between the civil authorities and the faithful. These preachers have no official links with foreign governments. Whatever their social origin or personal past, they are all quite familiar with the problems of youngsters from immigrant families and the social conditions they live in.

This search for meaning by a minority of immigrant-background Muslim youths and their interest in Islam explains the success of the new preachers, whom some sociologists have dubbed the 'new Islamic intellectuals.' Olivier Roy[2] says these preachers approach knowledge by questioning the legitimacy of the state and even the society itself. 'It works,' he says, 'by taking control, through sermons in mosques, of areas that are not part of classic society and that the state has not brought under its influence.'

Such 'new intellectuals' are well aware of the problems of young Muslims and speak their language. The gist of their message is that people should exercize their rights and duties in the society they live in. While stressing the spiritual side of Islam – the idea of justice and solidarity – they encourage people to get involved in the society. They see their job as helping people who feel marginalized, out of place or socially unwanted to shed their anxieties.

Each guide or preacher also has his own network of influence and support outside the Muslim community and some of them, such as Tariq Ramadan who we are looking at here, have had disputes with the authorities.

Ramadan is a guide and preacher like others, but is much more than that. However you describe him, he regards Islam as a political ideology that applies to broad areas of social activity and he sees society in a political light. But in the European situation, he sees Islam – unlike fundamentalists operating in the Muslim world – not as a geo-strategic issue but a social phenomenon. So he is at the dividing line between the 'suburban preachers' and international fundamentalism.

His platform, though not formally spelled out, could be described as reforming society 'from below.' This is not new or original, but he presses it persuasively through his great charisma, which comes from his way with words, his teaching skills and his family lineage. Ramadan is the grandson of Hassan El-Banna, founder of the Muslim Brotherhood movement in Egypt in 1928, and the son of another historic figure of the movement, Said Ramadan, who was sentenced to life imprisonment by President Gamal Abdel Nasser and exiled to Switzerland.

Tariq Ramadan's ideas focus on the place of Islam and Muslims in Europe. He wants to explore how one can be a good Muslim in Europe today. The

[2] This is the term O. Roy uses in *Intellectuels et militants de l'islam contemporain*, edited by G. Kepel and Y. Richard, Paris, Seuil, 1990.

context of his thinking is important because 'Islam is not only in a minority but secularisation is to the detriment of all religion.'[3]

The West no longer thinks of itself as religious, but a sizeable number of people in Europe from Muslim cultures have for the past few years regarded themselves as a mainly religious community. Reactions to this have been many. Ramadan's response is based on rebuilding and rearranging religious behaviour based on spirituality and morality. He wants to combine strict obedience to the teachings of Islam with civic commitment. To people who have been cut off from their roots and are having a very hard time finding dignity and identity in integration, he is 'offering a set of arguments and his own voice of authority.'[4]

Franck Frégosi sees him as 'a modern neo-fundamentalist doubling as a charismatic leader who puts his case in an informal and individual way, using stories of personal experiences, along with trust, advice and protection.' So he appears as 'a brother in Islam' who largely replaces the discredited father, the parent whose authority and image is waning.

Surveys among young people who flock to the courses and lectures he gives regularly in French and Belgian cities show they feel a special relationship with him. The religion they say they practice and have chosen to display openly is for most of them, except those who have been converted, in line with their social origin. It is the religion of a father who they say was not able to pass it on as a broad identity and heritage. So it is a bit like the religion of the father without the father. Ramadan is taking over from him to pass on the religion in its broadest sense. He gives his flock pride by presenting their religion as a heritage that has made its contribution to the world's culture and so gives them the means to defend themselves against any humiliation they may be subjected to.

Ramadan comports himself like a classic father, attentive to his offspring and taking a firm and disciplinarian attitude. Doubt has no place in what he says. Like a father, he has only beliefs and certainties while at the same time being protective. By alternating firmness and affection, he establishes, perhaps unwittingly, a fatherly relationship with youngsters. A relationship based on authority, affection and protection but also education and teaching. So you could say he has gone beyond his role as a guide and marked himself out from other preachers. But what really sets him apart is that he has various claims to legitimacy.

The first, a charismatic one, comes largely from his talents as a remarkable popular orator. He has a truly silver tongue and uses simple, clear, well-constructed language, speaking in the style of a storyteller and teacher. He also has the knowledge and ability to interpret Islam. He has built up his social authority by attracting followers whose behaviour he guides. Unlike other leaders who have emerged in Europe, Ramadan has a good knowledge of classical Arabic as well as his silver tongue, freely mixing references to Montesquieu,

[3] O. Roy, *op. cit.*, p. 70.

[4] This is F. Frégosi's expression, in 'Les contours discursifs d'une religiosité citoyenne: laïcité et identité islamique chez Tariq Ramadan,' in *Paroles d'Islam,* edited by F. Dassetto, Paris, Maisonneuve et Larose, 2000.

de Tocqueville and Rousseau with quotations from the Koran. He has the special art of reading passages aloud and seems to know the theological structure. He describes himself as a philosopher, but can also adapt the message of the Koran to produce a set of rules applicable to individual and community behaviour.

His second legitimacy is his lineage. He talks about it openly and even stresses it but denies any official link with the Muslim Brotherhood, which was a pioneer of the whole Islamic movement as such. The Brotherhood is seen as the first organised political expression of the Islamic reformism that sprung up at the end of the 19th Century in reaction to the West's technological superiority and political and cultural dominance. In Egypt, the movement first appeared at a social level, where it is most active. It only moved into politics in the 1940s and notably took part in the first Palestinian war. By the time Nasser and the Free Officers' Group seized power in 1952, it had a large network of more than a million followers. The Brotherhood fervently supported Nasser but he eventually rejected and cracked down hard on them. El-Banna was murdered in 1949 and another leader, Sayyed Qutb,[5] was hanged in 1966.

Ramadan, who fiercely defends his ideological and financial independence and condemns violence, does not go along with all the ideas of the Brotherhood, so his use of the connection is selective. Listening to him or reading his writings,[6] he is clearly the grandson of Hassan El-Banna, whose notions of social justice he highlights while playing down the global aspect of Islam. He makes very little mention of Sayyid Qutb because of the break he advocates between Islamic societies and others. Yet because of his lineage, Ramadan definitely has a historic legitimacy that involves both belief and militancy. As part of the family whose chief founded the Muslim Brotherhood, he seems to want to tie the Brotherhood's thought to Muslim reformism. This link-up means he can give the Brotherhood scientific legitimacy while removing the violent reputation it has in the eyes of many.

Ramadan says activity by 'committed Muslims' is part of the movement's continuity, along with the work of reforming religious thought, reviving spirituality and returning to the source, as a path to social action and a political alternative.

Apart from legitimacy through charisma and lineage, Ramadan is not really an alim in the usually-understood sense. He has no legitimacy through special scholarship. His knowledge of the holy scriptures seems accurate and well-expressed, but it is based on what he has lived. So he never interprets Koranic verses in absolute or timeless terms, but always in relation to the daily life and experiences of his audience. He believes that 'the teachings of Islam and the

[5] In 1965, Nasser was grappling with a number of problems and brought the Muslim Brothers back into the public eye by accusing them of plotting against him. Sayyed Qutb, the movement's ideologue, was sent to a detention camp were he wrote a sharp Islamic attack on Nasser's regime. He believed Islam should radically separate itself from the societies of that time. This desire for such a break was unusual and not in line with the attitude of most Muslims of the period, including the Muslim Brotherhood.

[6] T. Ramadan, *Aux Sources du renouveau musulman, d'Al Afghani à Hassan El-Banna: un siècle de réformisme islamique*, Paris, Bayard/Centurion, 1998, p. 478.

European environment must both be taken into account to produce serious thinking about all sensitive subjects.'[7]

Islam and citizenship

As a very aware Muslim, Ramadan feels he has a mission because these days Muslims often have a distorted view of themselves and thus of the Islamic way of life, to the point of forgetting what Islam is and how it has contributed to human civilisation. With such an attitude, it is hard for Muslims to imagine they have anything to offer the West. How can they play an active part in European societies and have a positive influence through an involved and respectful coexistence? Ramadan's aim is to 'integrate the individual while respecting religious and cultural characteristics in exchange for broad prior acceptance of the laws of the host country.'[8]

Ramadan says Europe seems to be a place where Muslims can live securely with guaranteed basic rights. As a minority in a non-Muslim environment, they can practise and respect the most important parts of Islamic teaching. So they have a wide and significant margin for manoeuvre – the right to worship which is guaranteed by law throughout Europe, the right to knowledge, the right of free association and the right to have organizations representing the community. But alongside these entrenched rights, there are others to be fought for, such as the right to an identity, which involves cultural obligations.

The state authorities must take these elements into account in devising an alternative plan for integration that would be midway between the Anglo-Saxon community-based version, with its risk of marginalisation and creating ghettos, and the French assimilationist model which takes no account of cultural specificity. Such a compromise would enable integration of a person while respecting their cultural and religious characteristics as long as they first agreed to respect the broad rules of the host country. This is what Ramadan calls positive integration and he does not see it as incompatible with laicity.

The approach means defining a new Muslim identity that no longer refers back to the country of origin but affirms an essentially religious kind of identity. A reconstructed or revised identity such as this has the advantage of 'freeing' Muslims living in Europe from a traditional culture linked to their country of origin that no longer makes any sense in their new European surroundings. By distancing itself from the old customs, from the histories of the original and the host country and from the disputes between the two of them, this reconstructed identity becomes universal and is also better adapted to European conditions.[9]

The new identity cannot be forged outside reformism, without a search for an authentic Islam that has been purified and simplified. Separated from the

[7] T. Ramadan, *Etre musulman européen,* Lyon, Tawhid, 1994, p. 293.
[8] T. Ramadan, *Les Musulmans dans la laïcité, responsabilité et droits des musulmans dans les sociétés occidentales,* Lyon, Tawhid, 1994, p. 92.
[9] O. Roy, *op. cit.,* p. 72.

country of origin, the revised identity blends better with citizenship. This is where Ramadan's role is important – redefining an identity broadly based on Islam – and is the key to his public popularity.

Ramadan's audience does not extend to all young Muslims in France and in Europe. His public is a section of them who have problems integrating. Contrary to popular belief, it is not youths from very poor city suburbs, but mainly people in the city itself from the rising middle classes who find their social advance blocked. Some of them have done quite well but have gained no recognition and have not managed to shed their frustrations. Most[10] are social Muslims, unsure of their identity, who feel Ramadan's message will enable them to become quickly and easily both good Muslims and good citizens. An educated public but not necessarily a scholarly one.

Another popular view, that his followers are very young, is also wrong. His audiences are usually people between 30 and 45 who, if they are not members of a religious association, often used to be.

These young people are not looking for a learned discourse on Islam from Ramadan. Their expectations are not clear, but they seem to find in this non-traditional preacher's message a way of expressing their cultural difference in a way that Westerners take notice of.

Ramadan uses emotion and charisma and mixes old and new teaching methods to win over a public that likes him for being himself, because he fills a gap, because he uses simple language and talks about local, everyday things in a European setting. His message is strongly political. He attacks dictatorships in the Arab and Muslim world but also stresses spiritual and moral issues, as well as the search for human dignity and personal fulfilment in relationship to God and the licit and the illicit. This is what Ramadan calls 'Muslim humanism.'

Ramadan has not been appointed by any higher authority and is not bothered by institutions or state structures, so is he helping create practices and attitudes in terms of norms and values that could be adopted by governments? If so, by integrating Islam, Europe could become an example of a new relationship between religion and politics. Muslims could then be the first to claim European citizenship for want of finding their place in national contexts. If this happens, the French-style civic ethnicity could be overtaken, as Franck Frégosi suggests, by an 'active religious-based ethnicity.'[11]

[10] His audience also includes converts.

[11] F. Frégosi, *op. cit.*, p. 219, quoting V. Geisser in *Ethnicité républicaine, les élites d'origine maghrébine dans le système politique français*, Paris, Presses de Science Po, 1997.

Index